INDIAN DAWN

INDIAN DAWN

JOHN S. HOYLAND

GYAN

Published by

Gyan Publishing House
5, Ansari Road
Daryaganj, New Delhi-110002
Phone: 011-47034999, 9811692060
E-mail: books@gyanbooks.com

Distribution Network
gyanbooks.com
India, USA, Canada, UK, Australia

ISBN: 978-93-7169-263-2 (PB)

First Published, 1934

2nd Impression 2025

Printed at: Gyan Press, Delhi.

INDIAN DAWN
Author: JOHN S. HOYLAND

INDIAN DAWN

BY

JOHN S. HOYLAND

CAMBRIDGE

W. HEFFER & SONS LTD

1934

CONTENTS

FOREWORD

THIS book has been prepared from matter written in intervals of time salvaged with difficulty from the manifold activities of a missionary life, primarily with the purpose of clarifying and expressing thoughts which have come into the mind of the writer during periods of prayer and meditation, generally in the early morning.

Most of the matter is now reprinted from the following: *The Fourfold Sacrament, The Sacrament of Common Life, Prayers for a One Year Old, Prayers for a Two Year Old,* and *The Sacrament of Nature.*

J. S. H.

WOODBROOKE,
April 18, 1934.

I.

THANKSGIVING

SECRET MARRIAGE

Mary Burleigh, the eldest girl of an orphaned family, because of her home responsibilities found it extremely difficult to marry and settle down in the ordinary way and so, under the persuasion of Calvin Tait, she agreed to a secret marriage. She soon found herself involved in all manner of evasion and difficulties—the complications at last becoming extreme.

FATHER,
We thank Thee to-day for the open air—
For sunlight ablaze on forest and river,
For merry companionship all the day long,
For this wild free life of the open,
For flashing water to swim in,
For thirst and hunger and wearied limbs,
For deep sound sleep at the end of the day:

For these Thy gifts most goodly,
We thank Thee, our Father.

FOR mountains to climb,
For risks to be run on the crags,
For steep snow-slopes to be crossed,
For falling stones, and treacherous rock,
For the long hard fight to the top,
As a man goes alone, alone in this stern mountain-world,
Alone, with his single strength
Pitted alone against danger and death,
Alone with God on God's mountain peaks—
Ah God, for this strange sweet gladness of danger Thou givest,
For this stripping away of disguise and convention,
For this facing alone with Thee of Reality,
I thank Thee, I thank Thee.

THE night of heat and of stifling despair is over
at last:
And the dawn of coolness and peace,
Of greenness, of life out of death,
Has arisen upon us:

For the rain, for the rain,
For the first fierce shattering torrents of rain,
Goodly, generous, cool,
We—with all things that live,
Plants, beasts, birds—
O Father, praise and adore Thine ineffable name.

FOR the strength and peace of the trees,
We thank Thee, our God:

For their quiet unhasting growth,
For their stalwart and trusty friendship,
For their sociable neighbourly silence:

For their ancient calm on a windless day:

For their cheery, murmurous stir
When the breeze is abroad with its melodies:

For the quiet and sure revelation of Thee
Which they bring to our souls
As we sit thus silent amongst them,
We thank Thee, our God.

WE thank Thee, our God,
That though Thou art beauty—
And beauty fairer by far than ought of our human imagining—
Yet Thou art also strength:

We thank Thee that Thou art revealed
Not alone through the tender grace of the flower-crowned valleys,
Not alone through the meadow-freshness:
But here on the heights,
…ere where the tempests rage,
Where the grim rocks frown storm-scarred,
Where the venturesome pines are twisted and shattered:

…e thank Thee that here in the stark and terrible mountains,
…ere also Thou art to be known:

…nd we thank Thee, our God,
…hat here is Thy beauty of Strength,
…hy beauty of wild brown moorland, of perilous crag,
… mountain lakes lashed white by the headlong gale:

…e thank Thee that here is a beauty more pure, more austere, more divine,
…herein Thou art brought, very mightily, home to our souls.

AT last, after heat excessive by day
And worse, far worse, by night,
There is coolness again—
A breeze that is not, as those other winds were,
Harsh furnace-breath of the pit,
But mild and gentle and cool:

Aloft floats the long bright banner, the Milky Way,
With Saturn ablaze, a silvery lamp, at its side:

In the South, lies the glow from a forest fire
Hidden afar beneath the horizon,
Yet clear to be seen in the fierce red light which it casts
On the mighty columns of smoke which it flings to the
sky:

God be thanked, God be thanked,
For His goodly gift of the night,
Our refuge and stay from this Indian sun.

FOR narrow paths through tall-growing corn,
For sunlight on far-away hills,
For cool shade of trees in the noon-time,
For whispering leaves and murmuring streams,
For dew on the grass in the forest,
For merry shouting of birds,
For strength to walk and for eyes to see, in forest and
field,
For Thy love shown forth so clear in it all,
We thank Thee, we thank Thee, our Father, this day.

FOR the dew on the grass we thank Thee, O Father,
Flashing with varied splendour
As the sunrise burns on the forest:

For the stately trees,
Dim seen at first in the dawn,
Then standing forth clearly on every hand,
Instinct with Thy peace:

For the rose-tinted mists in the hollows,
For the distant hills, blue and mysterious:

For the chirp of awakening birds,
For the secret romance of glade and of woodland pathway,
Vanishing into the shadows ahead, or across the hill's shoulder:

For the silence, most of all for the forest-silence,
The silence which is in itself Thy voice in this forest-world,
Speaking Thy secret of love to our souls,
We thank Thee, we thank Thee, our Father.

I THANK Thee, O God, for the ploughman,
Aloof and placid at his ancient task:
Behind him, the distant hills heave their long low shoulders
Far o'er the upland curve of the rich red tilth:

Blue are the hills to-day.
Blue with the rain that is gone, and the rain to come:
Peaceful and very still are the hills, as the evening falls:

Slow treads the ploughman,
Before him the oxen pace steadily on,
And the soil turns smoothly up from the ploughshare:

Above him, the birds wing home to their rest:

For this peace,
For this slow immemorial peace of the ploughman—
Man alone amidst Nature—
I thank Thee, my God, Who art known in it all.

FOR the sun-washed lake
Stretching away in long windy levels, cloud-barred,
To distant green hills
We thank Thee, our God:

For sudden gusts of soft rain, on the woodlands afar,
For the busy glee of the birds,
For the rough companionly clasp of the wind,
For trees astir and aswing,
For all this clean, goodly, joyful world of outdoors,
Away from man's crowding and hurry and petty restraints,
We thank Thee, our King.

FATHER,
We thank Thee this day for the open air,
For wide-reaching spaces, for desolate hills,
For measureless, empty sea,
For limitless plains, sun-scarred and bare,
For great rivers, so wide that their farther bank
Is lost in the mist:
For the long, straight, endless road through the forest,
For the million million trees of the forest,
Each a good friend,
For the host beyond count of Thy stars:—

For all this wideness and generous space of Thy world,
We thank Thee, our God, this day.

FATHER, I thank Thee, this day
For all the unspeakable beauty and joy of Thy forest-world,
For the sturdy and quiet friendship of trees,
For the keen delight of a perilous crag-climb,
Alone with Thee on the silent rocks:
For the coolness and still green depths of the water,
Fern-shadowed, cliff-walled :
For the busy clamorous life of bird and of insect,
For the stars by night—
For the sudden shattering storms—
For all things ancient and wild of the forest,
I thank Thee, I thank Thee, my God.

THE sky is an army this morning,
An army of dark and hurrying storm-clouds:

Here from our hill-top we see them,
In serried array, rank beyond rank,
Marching upon us at speed,
Passing us close,
Then marching swiftly away, to the East:

Thunderous dark though they be, these clouds,
They are welcome indeed:
For they bring us in generous measure
The rain, which is life after death,
God's rain to a sun-scorched land, blasted and barren
and dead.

FATHER divine,
We look up once more unto Thee
In this holy inviolate dawn:

We thank Thee for light renewed,
For a fresh day given, wherein to serve Thee,
For hard and exacting work to be done,
For a home to come back to, a perfect refuge from labour
and care,
For childhood around us, with its simple and trustful
joy,
For forest and hills,
For winds and for stars:

For all these unspeakable gifts that Thy love has
 showered upon us
We thank Thee and praise Thy name:

Give us power to love Thee and serve Thee aright.

SPIRIT of beauty and truth,
Spirit of purity,
Spirit of joy,
Spirit of life and power,
Maker and Builder of all that truly exists:
Spirit in whose holy presence within us
Stands or falls our eternal life:
Spirit of Christ,
Thou indwelling God,
Thou who art soul of our inmost soul,
Thou who art tenderness, friendship, comfort and love
Summed up in a Friendship, perfect, ineffable,
Thou who art Christ Within—
Here in the holy silence of dawn,
As the red glow kindles the East,
We stand to adore Thee:

We thank Thee,
We praise Thee:
But of all Thy gifts and Thy powers most do we thank
 Thee for this,
That Thou workest thus in a little child
To reveal God's beauty, God's glory, God's love.

FATHER, we thank Thee this day
For rest after labour—
For the forest around,
For the peace of broad spaces,
For song of birds and murmur of winds,
For golden clouds in the evening calm,
For silence under the stars:

Build up our lives in these simple unshakable things,
Give us always a secret source of quiet unharassed
power:

In the midst of the world's fierce turmoil,
In all these inconsequent hurries that fill our lives with
their clamour,
Give us hold on the forests and stars:

That beneath all activity
Peace may abide,
And be strong.

FOR water to swim in,
For the green forest-freshness,
God be thanked:

But, above all else,
God be thanked for the mountains;
For the great, white, terrible, beautiful mountains,
God's name be praised.

For there, on the white mysterious mountains,
God's Presence walks, and His Spirit is known,
With a keen and piercing assurance, in wonder and awe
and a trembling joy,
That are strangers to him who only may walk in the
valleys,
In the warm, safe, bountiful valleys.

God be thanked for the mountains.

THOU hast crowded my life with richness of love
and of joy,
O Lover divine, O joyful, most generous Giver:

Thou hast spoken with me in the dawn,
On the silent hills,
'Midst the waters that run in the hollow glens,
Through danger, through grief,
Through laughter of children, and sweet home-love:

Thou hast spoken in joy to my soul,
Thou hast held me and led me—a wayward and fretful
child—
Thou hast loved me through all:

O Master,
O wonderful, glorious God,
I thank Thee, I thank Thee, this day.

WE thank Thee, O God,
That, arising from sleep—
Sleep, the repose of our souls in Thy fatherly care—
We may plunge to this clear keen bath
Of radiant starlight:
And behold, as we gaze,
The systems beyond all number,
The order, the beauty, the peace,
Of Thy marvellous universe, fashioned after Thy will:

We thank Thee that silvery moon, flashing stars, and
the first red glow in the east,
Hymn thus aloud, in joy universal,
The praise of their Maker:

We thank Thee that our small souls
May join and be one in, be lost in,
That shout eternal of praise and of joy,
That communion of all these marvellous things Thou
hast made
With Thyself, their Creator.

BLUE lake-water,
Through the vivid green of the poplar-trees:
Pink wild-roses, down by the golden sand of the shore:
Blood-red poppies ablaze in the yellow corn:
Beside our tent a bank of blue iris,
And the dark green couch of their leaves.

On high, the dazzling snows of Kashmir,
And beneath them the black rock-ridges,
Crowned with their sombre pines.

Along the lake-margin
A kingfisher flashes, blue wings, yellow bill,
Orange breast:

Over all, the deep blue dome of the sky.

In all this profusion of colour, this wealth of beauty and joy,
Thy praise is proclaimed, O Father, Thy praise is proclaimed.

FATHER, we thank Thee to-day
For the essential underlying goodness
Of human nature.
We thank Thee that simple faithfulness and courage,
Kindness and love,
May find an echo, rouse a generous response,
In every heart:
We thank Thee that thus patiently and surely
Thou workest out Thine own unfailing purposes,
Thou buildest in the hearts of men
That Kingdom of Thy truth and love
For which Christ lived and died,
For which Thou callest us to live and die.

FOR laughter,
God's name be praised:

God's name be praised
For cheery companionship,
For old recollections revived
Of labours and joys and dangers gone by.

For the humour, the genial good-will,
Of everyday friendship,
God's name be praised.

For music,
God's name be praised,
Music that lifts a man's heart from earth
And flings wide the portal of heaven:

And for song,
The gracious flower of perfect song,
God's name be mightily praised.

TEN thousand feet below us
Young Sutlej shouts in her narrow gorge:
No sound of her deep insistent clamour
Reaches us here.

Eastward, soars from the valley,
Glacier-flanked, girt with gigantic cliffs,
Crowned with resplendent snows,
A single perfect peak of the main Himálaya.

Far to the left lie the smoky plains,
Shrouded with stifling dust,
Scourged by the sand-storms of May.

Far to the right lie the ramparts of Tibet,
With the twin red peaks of Leo
Guarding that perilous portal
Where Sutlej has broken her way to India.

Sixteen thousand feet in air we stand;
Yet, amidst these giants,
Our peak is as nothing.

Far north-westward, south-eastward,
Summit beyond summit,
They march—the world's supreme mountain-range.

Right in their heart we stand,
These steely and terrible summits,
These visions of beauty beyond belief,
These dazzling spaces of splendour and light.

Thanks be to Thee,
O our God,
For Thine own revelation,
In these silent and beautiful peaks.

THUS to sit silent together,
The day's work done,
Is very Heaven on earth.

Thus in silence to lift up our hearts,
Till there rises in each,
With knowledge imperious, absolute,
With joy ineffable,
The certainty of God's own craftsmanship
Moulding our souls to a new united being:
This, this is eternal life.

FOR the beauty and joy of Thy world,
Our God, we thank Thee this day:
For mountain and cloud,
For sunlight and forest,
For the great simple things
Wherein through silence Thou art revealed.

Still, we pray Thee, our hearts before Thee:
Give us silence, simplicity, peace,
That our souls may rise and expand
Upward to Thee.

Make us single-hearted and true,
As are these Thy great and simple and silent things,
Mountain and cloud,
Sunlight and forest.

WHAT a year this has been,
Little son:

From puniest weakness, to strength that daily increases
beyond all believing:
From moveless inaction, and power only to wail,
To a song unending of riotous joy,
A perpetual sunshine of laughter,
Energy, action unceasing:

From a being so frail that we scarce could believe thou
wouldst live,
To this quicksilver zeal for discovery,
To this magic emergence, day after day,
Of new and miraculous powers:

God be thanked, God be thanked,
For this radiant year:

And God grant, in the future,
With His ever-increasing bounty,
Energy, power, wisdom and joy.

WE thank Thee to-day,
Strong Saviour and Friend,
That our lives lie open and plain
To Thy piercing vision,
That our souls are naked
Before Thy majesty.

We thank Thee that in Thy sight
All pretences are stripped away:
That we, Thy children, are known most surely for
what we are,
Not for what we may seem:
That we face unsheltered
Thyself and our own true selves,
With no protecting convention or disguise,
Judged and condemned
By Thy keen and piercing purity.

We thank Thee that thus all illusion
Is daily rent from our souls,
So that, morning by morning,
We know ourselves to be mean and filthy and sin-
smeared,
For ever unworthy of Thine unwearying love,
For ever dependent, in weakness and shame,
On Thy power, Thy cleanness, Thy grace.

LORD of our souls,
We give Thee our deep-felt thanks this day
For the sacred communion of those who love Thee,
Both in Heaven and earth.

We thank Thee that heaven and earth,
For those who love Thee,
Are joined indissolubly
In one unbroken glory
Of Thy companionship.

We thank Thee that all our doubts are banished a world
 away
By this strong knowledge of Thy love,
That all our problems are solved,
All our sorrows and pains are clearly shown forth
In their own true nature, Thy method of drawing our
 souls to Thyself.

We pray Thee to-day for a knowledge more deep and
 joyful
Of these Thy great truths:
Above all we pray that our friendship with Thee,
And in Thee with those who abide perfected in Thee,
May go forward for ever from glory to glory.

LAST night, ere he slept,
His mother, returning, gave to our baby, already
 in bed,
A new toy,
A ball which rang with queer sounds when he shook it:

He laughed with delight,
He hugged his new ball,
He tossed it from side to side of his cot,
He shook it and rang it with shouts of ecstatic glee:
And at last he lay sleeping,
Still closely hugging his toy.

Our Father, we thank Thee,
That thus unto us it is given
With such simple ease
To make joy in this sombre world—
Joy whose laughing delight
Sounds so clear to thy Father-heart,
And swells with such might
The paean eternal of praise to Thy name.

SLEEPY, my son?
Lay down thy head on my shoulder,
And rest:

O Father divine,
From Whom all fatherhood gains,
For ever, its nature and name,
From Whom comes each impulse in human hearts
Of tender and patient love,
I look up to Thee, in deepest thanks for Thy gift,
And in knowledge joyous, complete,
That thus also, when I am weary,—
Above all on the day when I sink to rest,
This world for ever behind me,—
I have only to lay down my head on Thy shoulder,
As Thou holdest me close;
And safety and peace shall be given, past all human
thinking,
In Thine own omnipotent love
For ever.

BLUE eyes, new opened, after a night's long sleep:
Small arms upheld, for his Daddy to take him:—
Son, a year ago thou wast not:
And now—
The light of our lives,
A star of radiant joy,
A fresh revelation, day after day,
Of God's beauty and love,
A link, ever more strong,
With that other world
Whose fragrance still hangs around thee,
Whose grace shines out in each movement,
Whose gladness salutes us
In each small chuckle of baby delight,
Each slow-lisped word of thy baby tongue.

God be thanked,
God be thanked for His own fair thought
Thus set into flesh, and born in our home.

WE thank Thee, O Father,
That Thou hast given to us, Thy creatures,
Thy glorious, terrible gift of freedom—
Freedom to make or to mar
Not our own lives alone, but the lives of others.

We thank Thee that thus Thou dost train us,
Not as pupils jealously watched by a harsh, stern-spirited master,

Not as weaklings pampered and spoiled by a doting parent,
But as men, free men,
Who must fight their way,
Suffer and labour and die,
In the long hard desperate struggle
For manhood and character.

We thank Thee that thus we must pay,
By our blood and our tears,
For this terrible, glorious gift of freedom—
Pay for ill-using the gift,
Pay for the errors and sins of others.

Aye, we thank Thee even for this,
The hardest and darkest of all our problems;
For even here we are paying for freedom,
The freedom of others:
And here, for ever,
Thou art Thyself by our side,
Bearing within us and with us the burden of sorrow and pain,
Heartening our craven spirit
By Thy stalwart courage and cheer.

For Thou too, Master, didst pay
The utmost bitterest price
For freedom—
Pay with Thy life for man's misuse of Thy gift.

THOU Life of our life,
How shall we tell our love unto Thee this day?
How shall we thank Thee for all Thy grace?

Thou fillest our life with good things,
Joy upon joy, beauty on beauty,
No end is there and no bound to Thy generous giving.

Not as a rich proud patron Thou givest,
Not as a haughty despot flinging his gifts to the abject,
But silently, gently, in secret.

And ever the greatest of all Thy gifts—
The boon a thousand times richer than all Thy boons—
Is Thyself,
Thine own heart of love,
That great true heart which fills and sustains the universe
Yet ever is beating, close and tender and warm,
Next to the human hearts that love Thee.

O God, our God,
We thank Thee and praise Thee this day.

II.

JOY IN GOD

BLACK trees,
The fierce red glow of distant torches,
The moon, parting the flying clouds to peep through,
Water like molten night,
Smooth as a cat's fur,
Soft as a child's cheek,
Warm and close as a kiss;

Against the faint sheen of the sky
A figure, dimly discerned:
Outward it leaps, and down, down,
To cleave, with scarcely a ripple,
The lake's dark, resonant surface.

Then the motion of it—
The long steady drive through that ebon mirror:
The slow thrust and recover,
With bladed hands:
The swift flash as we dive
Down from dimness to blackness,
Down from irresponsive air
To the warm embrace of the water:

Thus to swim, in the forest, together, at night,
Is to live indeed,
To be drunken and drugged
With the joy of living,
To quaff, and in long deep draughts,
God's sacrament of delight.

OUR Father,
Our hearts go out unto Thee this day
In thanks for the endless innocent gaiety
Of sunlight and birds,
Of sparkling lake-water,
Of deer at play in the forest meadows,
Of boughs swinging free in the wind,
Over countless miles of the forest:

We thank Thee, O God,
For all Thy jovial open-air world –
And far above all we thank Thee
For this the most precious of all Thy gifts,
For this small son of our own,
Yesterday five months old,
Lustily crowing and kicking with joy –
The joy of achievement long sought,
As at last he brings his pink toes, after many a fruitless
attempt,
Home to his mouth.

THE heavens flame with the splendour of sunset,
Range beyond range, the fiery mountains of cloud
Shine in a wild and passionate glory.

The long low hills to the westward,
Shrouded in forest, mysterious, silent,
Are bathed in effulgence, transfigured.

The last red rays of the dying sun
Pierce direct, from margin to margin, the cloudy
empyrean,
Sending a signal of triumph over the world.

All this splendour is Thine, O our God:
Kindle our spirits ablaze with the glory of service for
Thee,
With the fierce and passionate joy of giving our lives to
Thy cause,
As the dying sun sets the heavens alight with the flame
of his death.

HOMEWARD, along the lake's dim reaches,
We drive our canoe:

In steady and disciplined lines
The crisp-cut ripples pass us, racing ahead,
And behind us the breeze blows shrewdly down from
the snows.

Purple-black lies the water,
So clear that by day
In the shadowy depths below
The swift-glancing fish and the feathery weeds
Are plain to be seen.

Before us, with crooked flight,
Scarcely discerned in the gathering dusk,
A bat flits hither and thither.

Next, a great owl,
Noiselessly beating the air with her soft-feathered
pinions,
Floats overhead, crossing the new-born stars.

The farther shore, with its stately plane-trees,
Is nought but a low black line,
Not even the white of our tent to be seen.

Then faintly, from over the lakes far vistas,
Comes stealing the sound of a song,
And a *vina's* thrum:
A lamp gleams, flickering dim,
From a peasant's home.

O moments holy, eternal,
O tender and beautiful heart of our God.
Alive in it all,
Whispering low to our souls
Thy love in it all.

MANY are the wild free joys of the world,
The joy of diving beneath great breakers
And of swimming stalwartly out to sea:
The joy of swift galloping over a sandy plain:
The joy of climbing up and up, across virgin snow,
To a solitary heaven-soaring peak of the Himálaya:
The fierce wild joy of an aeroplane's swoop,
When the heart exults in the sovereign glory of flight.

But keener than these is the joy of this work we share
now:
The grim mysterious joy of this struggle with death and
despair.

Ah, to have fought thus shoulder to shoulder,
To have carried together our share of the weight of
the famine,
To have faced together the blast of the cholera,
Each well knowing that help there is none,
If we sicken ourselves;
That die we must swiftly, here in the waste,
Untended, undoctored, tormented, befouled,
As thousands are dying around.

Ah, thus to have fought, and shoulder to shoulder,
To know that together we rescued a few from the foe—
Thank God for this joy supreme.

THY beauty shines, O God, through all created
things:
In all this wide immeasurable universe,
Thou art expressed, revealed,
Brought close and intimate and near:

Thy love, most mighty and most sweet,
In song of birds, in sunset-clouds,
In flower, in wind, in star,
Is eloquent, and tangible, and close.

Our God, how beautiful Thou art!

Ungainly, foolish words!
How can mere words,
The mask and darkening of reality,
Express Thy Being?

How can words, mere words,
Set forth Thy praise?—

And yet these hearts, they know a little,
These foolish hearts, they love a little,
Are rent and seared by love of Thee:

Strong agony of love,
Strong joy of love,
Because Thou lovest.

THE Joy of Thy heaven dwells in our hearts to-day,
O humble King of all worlds:
We hear—and hearing are ravished with delight—
Thy secret harmony,
The swing and lilt of that strong melody
Whereby the stars are ruled,
Whereby the planets circle in their right array,
Whereby the sacred dance of night and day,
Of summer, winter, life and death,
Is modulated duly
To the rhythm of thy Will.

We hear, from afar—
Yet clear and keen as the cry of the night-bird from the
    sleeping forest—
The song of Thine eternal triumph,
The song of Joy unspeakable and past belief,
The song of those who dwell for ever,
Thy work on earth well done,
In blissful union with Thyself.

TO meet Thee afresh,
O Lover divine,
Is to behold, at last, dawn after midnight darkness.

As we kneel here before Thee,
Giving the day most joyfully into Thy hands,
The breath of Thy presence
Sweeps, like the living dawn-wind,
Through our shut and stifling souls.

The night falls from us, as we meet with Thee,
We live anew, as thus we look upon Thy beauty,
As thus we take, with eager hands,
Thy gift, Thyself.

So send us forth, to work, all the day long,
For Thee,
Living Thy life, seeing with Thy eyes,
Striving, through Thy great power,
To build Thy Kingdom.

ALL the earth rejoiceth together,
With a joy unshadowed by pain or by death.

Mountain and swift-rushing stream,
Far lake-water under the moon,
Snow-peaks cleaving the heaven on high,
Sunlight and deep cool glades,
Birds in their free and innocent merriment,
Blood-red poppies that burn in the corn,
The fluttering moth, the deer on the hill,
Aye, and even this heart of mine,
All sing to Thy praise, their Maker and Friend.

YOU deny the existence of God?
Look forth on those forest-clothed hills,
Hark to the song of the birds,
Gaze up at the stars in the night,
Hear the call of the children at play.

Why, the world is resplendent with God:
His glory cannot be veiled:
Through the garment of matter it shines,
As the sun through a curtain of cloud.

Man needs but the listening ear,
But the eye that is willing to see:
With these he shall know and be glad
In the living assurance of God.

THE strength of the flood, the roll of the thunder,
the crash of the storm-blast—
All these are His own:
The quiet glory of dawn, creating the earth anew,
This also is His.
The rich dark splendour of starlit night, space beyond glittering space,
The mist on the river, the shadow of clouds on the mountain, the gleam of the sun-kissed lake,
The song of the birds, the murmur of wind in the tree-tops, the sound of the streams in the night,
All are His own.
In all things lovely He lives and speaks to our soul:
Yet more than in any of these is His glory set forth
In the sweet human love, tender and dear beyond words,
Which so richly He scatters abroad in our life.

Thanks be to Thee, O Lover and King;
May we faithfully serve Thee this day.

AT the end of a week of rain,
A week of darkness, gloomy and drowned and black,
The clouds have lifted at last,
And the sun breaks through.

Afar are the mighty Hills,
Thus seen at length after many days:
Clear-cut they shine on the azure heaven,
Their snows white-gleaming as never before.

Hark, how sweetly the birds rejoice,
Greeting the Sun with exultant shouts,
Darting from tree to tree in ecstatic bliss,
Towering aloft, or sweeping in swiftest flight down the
stream.

All God's creatures are glad:
The flowers lift up their faces again,
And the trees, resplendent in fresh-washed green,
Are fair new fanes set up to His praise.

So also my soul
Rejoices anew in Thee, O my King,
Rendering deep-felt thanks
For the manifold gifts Thou hast given.

FROM this crest of the wave of time,
Flung aloft from the depths for a moment,
Poised so briefly,
Soon to slide back and be gone,
Yet masters now for this moment
Of past and future—
All of the past centred and shaped to our hand,
The future helpless beneath the power we hold
To change it for good or for evil—
From this our brief, sharp, sovereign, splendid crest of
the wave,
We Thy creatures, O Father,
Give Thee our thanks for our being.

Swift we are vanished, forgotten;
Yet by Thy grace, for Thy glory,
We, the work of Thy hands,
Have been,
Have looked forth thus on Thy goodly world,
Have grasped in our hands past and future,
Have held them defenceless beneath our sway,
Have exulted in sunlight and mountains and seas,
Have stood here erect, in the keen swift wind of eternity:

Thus standing erect on the crest of the wave,
Soon to be whelmed and gone,
We salute Thee, our God, and we give Thee thanks for
our being.

O HOLY Light of God,
Shining from the beginning,
Guiding our race upwards from the brute,
Ever radiant through despair and death,
Ever undimmed and splendid in the darkness,
Shine Thou to-day in this dark heart of mine.

O holy Love of God,
Perfectly revealed,
Incarnate in this human flesh,
Dying for our life,
Suffering eternally our pain and grief,
Striving eternally for our perfection,
Work Thou to-day in this weak heart of mine.

O holy Joy of God,
Sharing the gladness of the least of all Thy creatures,
Rejoicing endlessly in honest laughter, and in gallant
scorn of death,
Taking delight immortal in all sweet human beauty,
Filling the world with the music of brooks and of birds,
Be jubilant to-day in this dull heart of mine.

O Thou great Heart of God,
Beating so closely to my own,
Sharing with me, even with me,
Thy Light, Thy Love, Thy Joy,
I thank Thee for Thyself:
Live Thou to-day in this dead heart of mine.

SPIRIT divine,
Spirit eternal of life and of love,
Striving for ever to tear Thy way forth
(Like a drowning man sunk deep in miry waters)
From the iron bonds of necessity,
From the fetters of space and of matter,
From the grip of the beast,
Into conscious and active loving:

God of joy and of light, Who lovest our souls unto
death and beyond,
Spirit of power,
Oh shake Thyself free, in us this day, from all that
hinders Thy full self-expression.

GLORIOUS as the dawn art Thou,
O Thou Light of our souls:
Glorious as the Indian dawn,
As it rises resplendent, beyond the dark hills and the murmuring forests.

Beautiful and peace-giving art Thou,
O Thou Rest of our souls,
As the Indian evening,
When the sun sets flaming through feathery cloud-bars,
And the world is transfigured in splendour.

For what are the dawn and the sunset
But Thine own deep thoughts of beauty and peace
Incarnate in colour before men's eyes?

Therefore, O King, we praise Thee and thank Thee this day.

PERFECTION of sweet and innocent beauty,
Set, by God's grace,
In frail mortal flesh:

Music of tiny feet to and fro:
Laughter, or April tears:

Each movement, each turn of the head, each step,
Each lissome, unconscious posture of grace,
A flash of the radiance of heaven.

Aye, as I see thee, my babe,
I rejoice with one glimmering spark of the gladness divine:

God shares me His joy,
As He looks on the fruit of His labour in thee
And is glad, beholding the beauty of heaven
Thus clothed in the flesh He has made.

MILE after mile of green forest-wall,
Close hedging the road:
Mile after mile of cool leafy glades,
Lavishly spread with the fresh green grass,
Where a fortnight ago was a scorching desert of stones.

Mile after mile the glad songs of the birds,
The merry chatter of parrot and jay,
The long curving leap and the shout of the monkeys,
Each creature rejoicing aloud in life renewed
By the cool green wealth of the Rains.

Mile after mile of feathery boughs
Waving in joy of the strong wet westerly gale,
Mile after mile of soft low clouds overhead
And of heaven-sent misty showers,
Where a fortnight ago was the brazen glare of the hot-weather mid-day.

Mile after mile of the goodness of God.

AH the joy,
To turn from this world of pedants and knaves,
Where all a man's labour is wasted and spoiled,
Before it is done,
Yet for the honour and love of the work he must labour on:

Ah the joy,
To turn from the weary and meaningless round of routine,
Where a man is so swiftly entrapped and bemired and lost;

Ah the joy,
To turn from the failures and follies,
To this little home,
Where is bliss beyond telling,
Eternal and deathless reality,
Simple joy,
Love unclouded and white,
And the goodness and friendship of God.

MASTER,
Men ask us for some word of Thee:
How, oh how, shall we show Thee to men?

Gautama was pitiful,
Arjuna was gallant,
Harishchandra faithful.

Strong is Ganges in the flood-time,
Tender is a mother with her first-born,
Beautiful is dawn upon Himálaya.

Joyful is the first new rain upon the forest,
Sweet is a kiss given at last
To one who for long has hungered in silence.

Yet Thou, O God,
Yet Thou, O our God, art more, how infinitely more,
    than these
In pity, courage, faithfulness,
In strength, in tenderness, in beauty,
In sweetness and in joy.

For Thou art, unto us, immortally,
Saviour and Lover of our souls.

Help us to-day to speak of Thee in work for Thee—
To speak of Thee in life for Thee,—
To speak of Thee, O Master, as Thou art.

O SPIRIT of the Living God,
Work out to-day Thy task,
Creating in our gloomy world
Thy Light of Christlikeness:

Be swift, be jubilant, be mighty
To conquer shame and wrong,
To build Thy City,
To forge through Christlike souls
A future where the Will of God—
His Will of Christlikeness—
Shall fully be performed in all these souls Thou lovest:

Build here, in her, our little child, to-day,
Strong Spirit of God's love and joy,
Thy City—
That fair and gracious City of true Christlikeness,
Build it in her.

CHRIST,
Joy of this feeble heart:
Christ,
Light of this darkened life:
Christ,
Beauty, Courage, and Love:
Christ,
Saviour from shame and from death
Into radiance of life with Thyself:
Christ, O Christ,
Leader, and Goal of the led:
Christ, O Christ,
Perfect God, perfect man—
My life at Thy feet I lay,
To be lived for Thee, by Thee, in my flesh.

ACROSS the dark rocks, dripping and seaweed-
fringed,
The long slow breakers tumble and roar,
Flinging on high their broken life,
Fire-flecked, in masses of silvery spray,

Overhead, as the last of the daylight dies,
Laughs and rejoices the moon, with a wild, weird,
magical joy:
And one great star, her attendant,
Solemnly waits on her mirth.

Into the warm caress of the Indian Ocean
Slowly we glide:
A few strong resolute strokes, and we float,
Firm held in the grasp of the good salt water,
Gently lifted and swung in a safe cool cradle,
As each smooth roller marches in pride to its doom.

Around us flashes and sparkles the swift phosphorescence:
In a thousand shimmering facets the velvety waters
Gleam with the dazzling sheen of the moon.

O moments divine and eternal,
Perfection of wild unearthly beauty in sea and in sky,
Perfection of silky delight in the touch of the ripples,
Perfection of faery joy in the glamour of moonlit waters:

The thanks of our hearts unto Thee,
O God, Who hast given it all,
Who art known in it all.

WHEN our hearts are cold and dead,
Oppressed with the burden of trivial detail and wearisome routine,
Sluggish, indifferent, uninspired—
Then of a sudden,
O Thou Joy of our lives,
Thou comest Thyself, beautiful, strong and divine,
To stir us to gallant effort,
To condemn, by Thy stern self-giving, our own self-pampering,
To shake us by the whirlwind of Thy spirit,
To make life terrible and glorious,
Full of unimaginable opportunities,
Instinct every moment with decisions and duties,
Fraught with the eternal issues of Thy Kingdom,
Where to-day's faithfulness or sloth
Means life or death in an infinite series of to-morrows.

Yet, stern and tyrannous though Thy claims may be,
Imperial as is Thy sovereignty upon our lives,
Thou Thyself, O Lover of our souls,
Art for ever our all-sufficient recompense,
Our exceeding sweet solace and delight,
So that in serving Thee,
And so alone,
We gain full pardon, and the richness of Thy joy.

III.

THE SACRAMENT OF HOME

WITHOUT, steady thunder of tropical rain,
Strong croaking of frogs,
Shrill calls of numberless crickets:
Black night, starless, abysmal,
Nought to be seen,
Where the light strikes out beyond the verandah-edge,
Save a solid wall of swift-falling water.

Within, a cosy glow,
Dry clothes, hot food,
And afterwards, music
To lift me clear in a moment
From weariness, failure and sadness
To the wide peaceful realm of God.

God be thanked, God be thanked,
For a home.

WHEN I am sad
Through too much thinking of myself,
Then I will remember,
Trees in the sunlight,
Hills beneath the dappled clouds,
Indian stars,
This little child.

A SUNNY Himálayan hill-top,
The snows beyond and the pines around,
Everywhere anemones,
Blue as the sky's bright diaphanous blue,
Shining like stars in the green of the grass:

Among them,
Flower of the flowers,
Star of these stars,
A babe of six months,
Luscious and goodly to see,
A star indeed of babes:

God bless thee, our son,
God keep thee,
God make thee a star for Himself
All thy life long.

FROM this our joy,
Quiet, unseen though it be,
May heaven and earth,
And all the dwellers therein,
Be eternally blessed.

Nought do we ask for ourselves,
Only that God shall take of our gladness
And share it, a sacrament perfect and holy,
To all of His creatures,
That all may rejoice in Himself.

GOD keep thee this day:
God give thee His spirit of beauty and truth,
That around thee, wherever thou goest,
Loveliness, purity, joy,
May leap into splendid being.

God give thee a spring of immortal gladness,
Ever fuller and deeper:
God guard thee from harm:
God use thee this day for His Kingdom.

God kindle in thee, to His glory,
The flame of His indwelling presence,
That thy life may shine as a star:

God keep thee and bless thee this day.

(On the death of a favourite Bull-terrier)

OLD friend,
True friend,
Farewell.

Long years we have chanced it together;
Through fair weather and foul,
In the dull city-round,
On Himálayan snow-slopes,
'Mid the cholera, heat and despair
Of a famine-May
We have fared together, we two.

You never grumbled or shirked,
You were never bored or resentful,
You were ever ready for fun or for fight,
You were gentle and game to the end.

Aye, and you loved me too,
God bless you:
In fever, in grief and in loneliness,
You were a comfort, you were,
Old friend.

Shall not God,
Who is love, courage, faithfulness, loyalty, truth,
Speak to our hearts, and be heard,
In a being like you—
You, whose heart was pure gold,
Whose nature and soul—
Aye soul—
Was compact, through and through,
Of love, courage, faithfulness, loyalty, truth?

Lie peacefully there,
Old friend,
With the lake beneath and the hills above,
And the scarlet poppies around:
Old friend, dear friend,
Lie peacefully there.

No more shall we climb together
Through the pines to the snow,
No more through the forest
Shall we fare forth together at dawn:
No more, in the soft still evening,
Wearied return to our tent.

Aye but I loved you,
Aye but I mourn for you,
God be thanked for you.

Old friend,
True friend,
Farewell.

LOVE is God's gift divine,
It is Himself:

Therefore when lives are utterly given one to the other,
All self-pleasing, all sordid desire, banished a world away,
Each heart taking joy in the other, with a flame of passionate gladness,
Each yearning, beyond expression, for the highest good of its comrade:
Then is God born anew upon earth.

Such love is Himself, creating with power purity, beauty and joy:
Such love is Himself, calling forth from the hearts of the lovers
Every gracious and goodly and heavenly gift:
Such love is Himself, purging the world from its hatred and wrong,
Founding in mystical fashion His Kingdom
Afar through His whole great universe.

Such love is Himself, undying and omnipotent.

A HOME
Is the armoury of God
In His battle to the death with evil, cruelty, lust.

A home
Is a tool to be used by God
In His own mysterious working,
To bring friendship and joy to the lonely and despairing,
To lift off loads of grief,
To block the mouth of Hell,
To fling wide the portals of Heaven.

A home
Is a treasury of God
Wherein purity, beauty and joy
Are stored, for His purposes, inviolate.

A home
Shall be potent
Through the world and beyond it
To scatter abroad the love and the knowledge of God.

For a home, a true home,
Is in itself the triumph of God,
Banishing Night and Chaos and Necessity,
Indwelling this lifeless clay
With the spirit divine of freedom and joy,
Overcoming to all eternity
Evil with Good.

TRUE love is born and exists
In a realm beyond this world,
In God Himself.

In God, and in God alone,
When our souls are silent before Him,
Can a voice, a caress, that is not of this earth
Make fitly known this fulness of imperial joy:

Therefore let us be silent before Him,
For in Him alone is the full and perfect expression
For this our delight.

PINK toes paddling in warm stream-water:
Above, the rich sunset-glow,
Birds flying homeward in swift joyous companies,
Everywhere long purple shadows,
Coolness, and evening peace:

A good and a glorious world lies before thee, my son,
Full of wild secret delight,
Blue hills, mysterious forests, cool leaf-shadowed waters:

God bless thee,
God make thee, all thy life long,
A man of the open air,
A man who exults in the wild free world,
Gaining therefrom deep peace, and renewal of life.

AH the joy to return
From the world's base ideals, its cynical follies:

Ah, the joy to return to this fortress, our home,
Stalwartly based on the living rock,
Garrisoned fast by the armies of God,
Four-square to the storms and the fierce assaults of the
foe.

Ah the joy to regain its portal
Sore-battered, far-spent,
Wounded and grimed in the conflict,
To listen at last to the clang of its postern behind:

Ah the joy to be safe,
Where peace and purity reign,
Where my soul has leisure to live,
And to taste again of God's love:

Ah the joy to kneel thus together once more,
To receive from the hand of the King
His free-given treasures of peace and cleanness and joy,
And to drink at His rich deep fountain of love.

AS thus I hold thee sleeping in my arms,
Small fragrant bunch of joysomeness and love:

As thus I ponder what those hands may someday do,
And where those ten pink toes may go:

I lay thee thus, all warm and soft and lovely,
In God's strong arms:

We dare not trust ourselves to care for thee,
To train thee as we should for Him:

But He will care, we know,
And He will train thee right.

We dare not trust ourselves with all this radiant beauty,
With all these boundless powers:

But God will keep them safe,
And God will teach us how to learn from thee
His deepest lesson,
His own simplicity and childlike trust:

So in His arms
I lay thee sleeping safely, whom I love so much,
My son.

FATHER, this day
For our home we pray Thee—
Our home, which, small and unknown though it be,
May yet most plainly show forth
Thine eternal glory.

May Thy love everlasting
Be reborn in our home this day.

May we take of the sacrament, all day long,
Of Thine own great love in the life of our home.

May we meet with Thee here,
May we know Thee here,
Be drawn very close to Thy side,
See revealed, in mysterious splendour,
Incarnate once more upon earth,
Thy life, Thy love, in our home this day.

Father, we pray Thee,
Give us grace for this highest and holiest task,
To build up a perfect home-life,
That shall give to Thyself, the Omnipotent God,
Power to create, through weak human lives,
Thine own perfection of love.

AT earliest dawn
As I stole on tip-toe past her bed,
With elaborate precautions not to wake her,
My little daughter lifted her head from her pillow,
Laughed aloud in delight as she saw me,
Then laid herself down once more to her sleep:

In that laughter
Heaven broke through on to earth,
Reality spake through the mists of our mortal delusion,
Spirit eternal took hold upon matter
And forced it to serve the ineffable ends:

I saw—even I, this weak human thing—
I saw, I heard,
I adored the Divine at work through the mortal,
The Love eternal creating the joyful splendour of heaven
Here upon earth:

I saw, I heard:
Thanks be to Thee, Father-God:
In her laughter I saw and I heard.

CHRIST,
Unworthy I am even to call on Thy name,
Yet deep in my inmost soul
I know, I know,
That Thou lovest,
That Thou, O Christ, art all love, summed and gathered
to one great love,
Pure, changeless, patient,
Strong, peaceful, wholly sufficient for all our need:

Christ,
Captain, Brother and Friend,
Here in Thy hands is my child to-day,
With her weakness, her strength of beauty, her need
of Thy guidance and care:

Bless her,
Keep her,
Make her, for Thee,
A Song, all her days, of goodly and generous joy.

TOUSLED head on the pillow,
Little plump arms stretched out for a good-night kiss,
And a child's sweet reticent love
Shown thus, in perfection, for me:

I thank thee, my little girl,
For this mighty, incredible lesson,
That the love which God feels unto man
Is the same, yet unspeakably more,
Than this great tide of love
Which even my narrow heart
Can feel for thyself.

BOTH hands stretched up to the sky,
Where the shade of evening has fallen deep,
My little son, scarce two years old,
Runs forward across the grass
With upturned face and baby clamour of delight—
For even now, for the very first time in his life,
He has seen the stars.

Thus also shall we rejoice, with a childlike delight,
When at last, O Father divine,
We behold the glory of Thy heaven.

Aye, and Thou also wilt share our joy,
More deeply joyful than ourselves.

WE ache for thy danger and pain,
Little son,
Danger and pain which we may not share,
Though sorely we long to take them and bear them:

All we can do is to come with our heavy need
To Him, to the Father,
To the Father who loves thee unspeakably more
Than we, even we thy parents, can love thee:

Safe then we lay thee, eternally safe,
In those safe strong arms.

SWEET flower of beauty and joy,
Strong voice of God to our hearts
Speaking His love, His long watchful care,
His will eternal of making such souls for His friendship—
May God's own work be perfectly done
In thee this day:

May His grace fill thy life,
Grace to grow rightly unto His praise,
Grace to reveal, in each action and movement,
God's gladness, God's love, to our darkened and groping souls
That have travelled so far from His simple discipleship:

Day after day, and ever more fully,
May God's likeness be kindled within thee, our son:
May God's will for His world work through thee unchecked and triumphant.

ALL her life long,
O Father of Love,
Make her a song of praise to Thy name:

May she move through the world revealing Thy nature
In simple, unconscious beauty and grace
Wherever she goes:

May there spring into being around her
Belief in goodness and truth,
Will to perform the right,
Hatred for ugliness, vice and brutality:

May this life of hers be a proof
To many a broken and desolate heart
That the Universe cares for man's need,
That sure and deathless and trusty
There dwells at the centre of all things
A Soul of beauty and joy,
A Heart of purity, goodness and love.

SHINE through this little life,
Thou holy Light of God,

Kindle in her Thy Christlikeness,
Use her to flash abroad Thy splendour,
To show Thy Light of Christ:

Here is this life,
So small, so frail,
And yet most beautiful, beyond all word:

Take it, O Father, for Thyself,
Be strong, be free in her:

Break down all hindrances,
And work Thy will,
That so, in this small life,
And far abroad through it,
Thy City may be built,
Thy Kingdom come.

FATHER,
Thy promise is sure,
That above all other good gifts
Thou wilt give, to him who asketh in simple faith,
Thy Holy Spirit:

Father,
We ask—
Thy children, here at Thy knee, in the dawn,
We ask,
Looking upward in trust to Thy face of love,
We ask,
Knowing that love of Thine to be better and deeper by far
Than the best and the deepest that father or mother can give,
We ask:

We claim Thy promise,
Thy Spirit on this our child:

Give her Thy Spirit,
Make her strong, pure, beautiful,
Make her a light in Thy world for Thee,
Make her a tool for Thy Kingdom,
Make her a power, a splendour,
Whom seeing, many shall turn unto Thee and be glad.

BE happy, laugh, chuckle, crow, cackle with gladness
to-day,
Thou bundle of frolicsome joyful delight:

Be a fountain of love and of laughter,
A beacon of joy in a sombre world:

Just a year old—
And what a year!
What a different world
In one short year!

And all this change in the world since one baby,
One fat and jovial baby,
Has been living and growing and loving,
Unnoticed save by a few,
Here in one small happy home:

God be thanked for thee, son.

EACH day sees some fresh skill gained,
Some new achievement made good,
Some conquest of spirit and mind
Over lifeless matter:

Yesterday, held between two of us,
Thou didst take thy first walk,
Toes firmly planted, chest flung stalwartly out,
Head proudly erect:

The day before that thou didst crawl,
To thy vast delight,
On hands and toes,
The ground untouched by thy knees,
Like a little bear:

To-day it is climbing,
All up the sides of thy cot, rail after rail, like a ladder,
Till over the topmast verge thou dost hang,
A fat, most kissable bunch, but in imminent danger of falling:
What will it be, I wonder, to-morrow?
God bless thee and guard thee and teach thee,
As thus thou repeatest, O son,
God's conquest in man over matter,
God's creation of freedom to mould stark necessity:

In all that thou doest, wherever thou goest,
All thy life long,
God bless thee and keep thee.

AS we watch thee thus peacefully sleeping,
Little son,
With thy baby hands, deep-dimpled, clasped tightly together,
And thy face close-nestled down to the pillow,
We see in thee—even in thee, so small and so weak—
The whole long future of man:

We see, as we watch thee,
Life wearing old, yet ever renewed in beauty and youth,
Life eternally young,
Life immortal, age after age down the future,
Life drawing ever more near unto God,
Life ever more wise and more strong to conquer necessity,
Life ever more free,
Life ever more pure to vanquish the base and the shameful,
Life ever more lovely, shot through with the splendour of heaven,
Life ever more childlike and joyful:

We thank Thee, we thank Thee, our God,
That these things shall be—
That age after age shall come nearer to Thee,
Shall behold Thee more clearly,
Shall commune with Thee ever more closely, heart unto heart:

Aye, we thank God for this lesson,
Taught, little son, through thyself.

SMALL sleepy head,
Downily soft,
Raised for a moment, thus at the earliest dawn, from
thy pillow,
To smile at thy Daddy,
Then dropped once more, with a drowsy sigh,
And asleep:

O my son,
God bless thee and keep thee this day,
God fill thy life with His love,
God grant that thy soul may lie open to Him,
Thy will be moved by His will,
Thy heart filled full with His joy,
To-day and to-morrow
And all thy life long:

God keep thee, my son,
God make thee His own.

NOT a letter,
A score of badly-spelt words,
Stained and smeared,
A poor little fragment of wasted paper.

Yet to me more precious than rubies,
For the writer thereof is my six-year-old son,
And he writes it because he loves me.

Thus also,
O Father divine,
Thou acceptest from us, Thy wayward children,
With joy, this gift of our lives:

Stained and wasted they are,
Yet thou wilt not reject:
For we bring them to Thee this day
Because we love Thee, and would show Thee our love.

A FRAGMENT of common wood,
Rudely hacked from a rough old plank,
Unplaned, unpolished, misshapen,
Deeply scored with uneven letters—
Yet how dear to my heart,
For on it my little son,
Six thousand miles hence,
With heavy labour of love,
Has cut for me
The one word "Daddy."

Even so,
On this rough life of mine,
Untamed, misused, and mean,
I would with heavy labour impress
In signs that shall never be lost
Thine own ineffable name,
O Father divine,
That Thy heart may rejoice.

FOR baby chucklings of delight
Here in the earliest dawn,
We thank Thee, Master and Lord:

Teach us to lead this babe and to train him aright
By Thy way, which is freedom and love:

Teach us, O Christ, to plant in his mind, his life,
Thine ideal of selfless activity:
Teach us to show him Thy joy in friendship, in beauty
of flowers and forest,
Thy belief in the infinite worth of each human life:

Teach us to train him to be what he was, from whom
he is named,
Francis.

RICH may thy whole life be with God's joy,
Little son,
Rich with His own deep love,
Rich with the splendour of losing thyself in His own
great cause:

Mayst thou have eyes to see, in His wonderful world,
The beauty of God revealed:
Mayst thou love with passionate joy
The dawn, the stars, and the mountains:

Mayst thou see God's truth,
And have power to tell it to men:

Mayst thou help our humanity forward
Far on the long hard road
That leads from hatred and strife to good-will:

Mayst thou burn like a fire
With zeal and courage and faith
For God and His Kingdom:

If pain and loneliness come
Mayst thou struggle forward undaunted,
Pursuing the truth:

Mayst thou fight to the end
God's battle for love and for right:

And if, at the last, grim failure betray thee,
Mayst thou still be stalwart, undaunted,
Thy hand in God's hand.

AS thou liest asleep,
Little son,
This hot and breathless night,
We drink in thy beauty with long deep draughts.

And we know, as we watch,
That each gracious line and curve of thee,
Rounded so softly, veiled so lovesomely
In the clear warm satin of thy skin,
Is shaped by the chisel of God,
Designed by His own creative artistry.

Never did human sculptor
Carve such perfection of outline and form:
Never did human artist
Devise such delicate blending of tint and texture and shade:
Never did human poet
Utter in human language a loveliness so divine.

With deep heart of joy
We render our thanks to the Sculptor who wrought thee so fair,
To the artist who limned thee so bright,
To the Poet, the Maker, whose master-thought
Created thee thus from the void.

GOD hold thee close to Himself,
This day and all days:

God save thee from loneliness, all the way on,
From stark desolation of spirit,
From hopeless, despairing famine of love.

God fence in thy life with His own great love:
God train thee and shape thee, in beauty and grace,
Unto a manhood wide-hearted, redemptive,
A manhood selfless, pitiful, Christlike,
That so, through thy life,
Love may break its way forth amongst men
And go forward in triumph undying.

IV.

TRUST IN GOD

ROUND about God,
The busy mind of man piles up the heavy adjectives,
Till He is hidden altogether from our sight—
Omnipotent, all-knowing, absolute,
Incomprehensible, ineffable,
Ruler afar, with all-controlling sway
Of a thousand thousand worlds unknown—
Howsoever thou shouldst know Him,
"Not that, not thus," they cry, His zealous worshippers.

But nought, and less than nought, care I
For all your adjectives,
For all your small officious zeal,
For all your cheap, high-sounding flattery.

This and this alone know I,
God loveth me, God loveth even me.

Here close His love enfoldeth me,
Here, close by mine,
I feel and know the throbbing of His heart,
The impulse of His strong eternal Will.

Here may I gaze
Up to God's face,
Finding therein love, sweetness, courage.

For God has claimed me as His child,
His weak unworthy child,
And yet his own.

FATHER, we thank Thee, this day,
That having Thyself, we have full and joyful assurance
That the best is for ever ahead,
That the joy of the future is more than the joy of the past,
That Thy presence shall teach us to grow, day by day,
In love, in courage, in strength,
For ever becoming more like to Thine own great pattern in Christ.

We thank Thee, that having Thee,
And being for ever held fast in the grasp of Thy love,
There can be, for us, no despairing failure,
Though our work may perish,
No darksome horror of oblivion,
Though our names be lost and forgotten.

For in Thee, and with Thee,
There is Life, Immortality,
Triumph at last, and perfection of Joy,
So that the feeblest and weakest and worst
May be saved and be stalwart for Thee, for ever.

NO words have I when you ask me of God:
He is, in Himself, all that my hungry soul craves,
All the beauty, the goodness, the truth and the joy of the world,
Summed up in a heart that beats here by my own.

He is my Captain, generous-hearted and true:
He is my King, swaying the stars by His word:
He is my Hero, who gallantly goes to the fight,
Against desperate odds, for purity, justice and truth.

He is my Friend, the desire of my heart.
Merry, companionly, staunch,
Faithful till death, and beyond.

The Light of my life is He,
The Joy of my soul:

Yet what are these foolish words?
How can mere words show one ray
Of God's beauty and glory and strength,
Of the heaven of life lived in Him?

WITH Him, in His home,
There is laughter and joy, and a ready welcome for all:

With Him, in His home,
There are merry voices of children at play:

With Him, in His home,
There is genial friendship of kindred hearts:

With Him, in His home,
There is simple abundance of all things needful and good:

With Him, in His home,
There is work, absorbing and hard, to be cheerfully done:

With Him, in His home,
There is rest and renewal of soul, quietness, leisure and
peace:

With Him, in His home,
There are riches of love for the loneliest,
Strong and redeeming and pure,
Triumphant for ever over sin and the grave.

And that home is each heart upon earth
Where entrance is granted to Him.

BLIND are we,
Blind from our birth,
Our eyes are darkened and dulled by the mists of the
world.

Yet shall we see,
O ye that have eyes at last, we shall see:
And the first that we shall see,
The first that ever our eyes shall behold,
Is the first that ye saw—
Is Thy face,
O Lover, O King,
Is the kingship, the love in Thy face.

We thank Thee, O God,
That for Thee is our sight reserved, set apart,
It is holy and sacred, for Thee alone.

O God, we shall see,
We shall open our eyes at last
On Thy face.

We shall see, we shall see.

AGE after age riseth before Him,
Age after age shall crumble and pass away:
Chivalry and wisdom, gallant self-surrender and devotion
Vanish and are gone.

In Him alone hath History her meaning,
In Him alone is hope and progress for mankind:
From Him we have come, unto Him we return,
Who is our Home.

Is the strife unavailing?
Nay, for Himself He fighteth beside us:
Foremost He is to dare and to die:
Himself in the wounded He groans, Himself He falls in
the slain.

He is the Captain, He rallies the ranks:
He is the Victor, He heads the assault:
With us and in us and for us He is sharing it all:
And at last we shall triumph with Him.

I THANK Thee, O Christ, for this moment,
Long-sought, brief-lived, but ageless and eternal—
This moment wherein Thy face is revealed,
The touch of Thy love comes home to my heart in joy,
And I know,
Beyond all argument, beyond opinion,
Beyond all faith,
Beyond all hope,
Beyond all knowledge,
I know:

I know Whom I have believed,
I am at peace, and confident,
In Him.

FATHER,
We trust Thee, we trust Thee:

In Thy care, in the grasp of Thy love,
All is safe, all is utterly safe:

Our souls shall commit unto Thee
That which is dearer by far than our life,
With certainty, unflinching, absolute,
That in Thy Home,
With Thee,
To Thine own children,
Never, through all eternity,
Can any harm come.

MASTER, I daily betray Thee,
Unworthy I am to kneel at Thy feet:
Neither goodness is there nor purity in me:
Nought but disloyalty, meanness, self-serving.

All things lie open to Thee:
Dumbly I show Thee the worst,
All my shame and my sorrowful weakness,
All my baseness and cowardice, failure and folly and sin.

O Master, beautiful, stainless and holy,
Thou knowest it all:
I am Thine, take Thou again
This worthless gift of my life,
Ah! take me again.

Only, O Master, O Christ,
Only, I love Thee so:
O Saviour, O Lover, O King,
I love Thee so.

HERE wait I in silence
For ninety slow minutes,
Whilst under the surgeon's knife
Fate is worked out—
Fate, whether that which I love a thousand times b
    than life
Shall die, or shall live.

Fate, said I?
Nay, here as I wait
(My soul gathered up and crouched at God's feet
In a long dumb anguish of prayer),
Of a sudden the barriers fall,
The curtain of sense rolls back—back—back,
And is gone:

Still do my eyes look out on the sunlight,
The song of the birds still comes to my ear,
And the slow deliberate march of the clock:
Yet my spirit is lifted clear of it all,
Clear from this fragile and changing world,
Beyond and away.

Around my soul
Lift and strain the tides of eternal life,
Lift and strain, and bear me away:
Around my soul
Thunders in slow majestic rhythm
The surge and beat of Thine endless love,
O Father—
Not Fate, O Father, not Fate, but Thy love.

O Thou, in whom all love
Is born, and for ever lives:
O Thou, who gavest this love,
Who rejoicest for ever in all true love:
Father, whose love for that single soul
Is love for a world of souls focussed and fixed upon one:
Father, upon whose bosom
Lieth that white soul now

(Mind dulled by the drugs,
Body shorn by the knife):
Father, in life and death
To be utterly trusted:
Father, Thy Will be done.

DARK waves on an iron-bound coast,
Huge, menacing,
Omnipotent in irresistible advance:
Yet each shall be shattered at last to silvery spray on the rocks.

The desert land,
Blackened and scorched by the fierceness of summer,
A horror of brazen glare, and famine, and death:
Yet at last the Rains shall come, and that land shall be green and shall live.

A long black night of the Rains,
No vestige of stars or of moon,
The earth close-veiled in the low-flying clouds:
Yet at last, sodden, belated, cometh the dawn.

The night of despair,
Of weariness past all telling,
Of heartache, loneliness, tears:
Yet at the last God giveth joy.

Long, and dreary, and bitter,
Is Thine anguish, O God, in creation:
Long and hard
Is the building up of Thy Kingdom:
Yet at the last Thou shalt triumph.

IN the rich joyous heart of the Indian night,
With the moon's white glamour quiet and clear overhead,
And the forest, dim-stretching,
Instinct and alive with mysterious silence:

When each tree
Is a fountain of shimmering fairylike beauty under the moon,
When each faint sound
A breaking twig, the croon of a sleepy bird—
Is a secret voice and a call:

When a man's sluggish heart is exalted within him,
When fifty dull generations fall swiftly away
And he hears as his far-off fathers heard,
Strong, compelling, bewitching,
The Call of the Wild:

Then be Thou by our side,
As we pass from glade unto secret glade
Through the magical sheen of the moonlight
And the black-dark caverns of shadow:

Be Thou by our side,
As we pass from our cosy lamp-lit tent
Into the wild new world of the forest-night,
Like souls, wondrously blest,
That fare forth together,
Away from this homely world of men—
But with Thee by their side—
Through the dim and radiant mysteries of death.

V.

THE FATHERHOOD OF GOD

FATHER,
Thy name be praised
That here and now, for Thy trustful children,
Thou makest this world a garden of secret joy:

Thy name be praised
That, hand in hand with Thyself,
We, Thy children, may wander on
Through the dim mysterious vistas of time.
Year after year,
Kept very safely each moment,
Guided and guarded, lest harm should befall,
By Thine own great love, each step of the way.

Thy name be praised,
That pain and sorrow but draw us more near to Thy side,
But teach us to clasp Thy hand more closely,
But prove to our souls more clearly
How dear, and how loving and strong Thou art.

Father, dear Father
May we trust Thee more wholly,
Till a glance up to Thee,
A silent pressure of Thy strong hand in our own,
Shall be all that we need, whatever befall,
To bestow on our souls, in all-sufficing perfection,
The knowledge of life eternal, in Thine own omnipotent love.

TAKE this Thy happy child to-night,
Strong Father and Friend.

As the moon tops the poplars
And lights, with her quiet radiance,
The swift-flowing silvery waters,
Where those poplars, even now in the night,
Are mirrored so clear, and with them the distant snows:
Take this Thy happy child,
O dear, dear Father and Friend.

It is time for sleep,
And Thy child comes again to Thy knee,
Sure of a perfect welcome,
Sure of forgiveness for failure,
Sure of a sweet deep sleep,
Safe held in Thy care.

Take this Thy happy child to-night,
Strong Father and Friend.

WARM baby arms round my neck,
A cheek, softer than down, pressed tight against mine,
And a voice whispering gently, "Daddy, I love you so."

A flower of joy art thou,
O my son,
A herald of love divine and the beauty of heaven.

Yet more than this thou art, my son;
For with authority most absolute
Thou teachest me, thy father,
That just as the clasp of thy arms round my neck
And the print of thy lips on my cheek
Thrill me with unspeakable delight,
So also—a thousand times more—
Doth God Himself rejoice,
When even the least and the weakest of us poor mortals
    His children,
Coming thus quietly unto His arms,
Brokenly tell Him our love.

Ah, if this mean heart of mine
Can thus break with love of thee, little son,
How vast is the heart of God,
Who loveth each human soul
With a love ten thousand times stronger.

IN the still dim morning
We worship the King.

From afar comes the voice of the wood-doves,
The call of a deer,
The steady drip from the leaves after a night of rain:—

Common things:
But ah how His heart beats through them,
How they flame with the splendour of God:

Each leaf of each tree is transfigured,
Each murmuring voice of His creatures
Is glad beyond measure
With the notes of His joy.

Father, Thy Life
Beats strong and divine through it all:
We need but to listen a moment,
And here is the throb of Thy heart
Close felt by our own:
Here is the voice of Thy love,
Here the shout of Thy triumphing love
Loud, loud in our ears.

LAST night, in fever and pain,
Thou didst waken, my son, most bitterly weeping:

And when I hastened to help thee,
Thou wouldst not be comforted,
Till at last I took thee up from thy bed,
And walked with thee, to and fro,
Without, where the great stars shone:

Then, in a moment, laying thy head on my shoulder,
With a sigh of content, thou didst find thy rest:
And I, thy father, thanked God from the depths of my
soul
For that joy which He gave—
The joy of knowing thy trust and thy love,
The joy of giving thee comfort and peace:

And I thank Him too that thus also,
When in trouble and pain I call out for His aid,
Beyond all shadow of doubt
He will be with me,
To lift me away, out under His stars,
Where His foolish and wayward child
May lay down his head on the Father's shoulder,
Be filled with peace in His love,
And trusting and loving Him
Rejoice His Father-heart with unspeakable joy.

I THANK Thee, Lord, to-day
For all my father taught me of Thyself,
For all he was to me of Thee:

I thank Thee for his patience and his love,
His wisdom, his deep genius for friendship,
His gentleness, his tenderness in strength:

I give Thee deepest thanks,
That now, when I am downcast or afraid,
One thing alone I need,
To tell myself once more,
"God is like that:
God cares for me, is eager to give all His best for me,
Even as my father cared and gave:
God loves, God patiently endures,
God is truth, wisdom, gentleness and strength,
Even as my father was, yet infinitely more":

Grant, Heavenly Father, this my prayer,
That some day my small child
May say one-tenth of this
About myself.

O REST unspeakable,
To turn from the clatter and drive of the world
To His peace.

O rest unspeakable,
To relax the strain,
To lay aside all bustling activity,
To repose in His presence again, in His silence and strength.

O rest unspeakable,
As my soul, released from this narrow cell,
Lives, and is free:

As I rise at last from this choking fog-bank,
And breathe once more the keen air of His heaven,
Knowing in silence the Truth.

O rest unspeakable,
To come to His knee as a child,
To look up in His eyes,
And to live again.

BY self-tormenting thou shalt never know Him:
By rite and ordinance thou shalt ne'er come nigh
Him:
Thy mighty-worded doctrines but proclaim aloud
Thine utter ignorance concerning Him;
Not by ceremonies duly done,
Not by works most piously performed,
Not by narrow-hearted creeds,
And not by dark austerities thou reachest Him.

Cease from all thine anxious careful searching,
And be a child again,
His child.

Come:
He calleth:
Come, as a child comes running to his mother's knee:
No doubt has he that she is there and loves him:
He only comes to her, in simple trust:
And lo, there in a moment he is safe,
Held strongly in her love.

Thus, thus is God:
Thou needest but a simple trust,
But a childlike heart, my soul,
And thou shalt know and feel and see
The eternal God Himself.

VI.

THE NEED FOR GOD

O FATHER, Father,
No prayer of any child of Thine,
However brief and crude, however feeble,
For ends however vast—
The righting of a world,
The coming of Thy universal Kingdom—
Can ever go unheard,
Can ever rest neglected and unanswered.

Thou art our Father and our God,
And when we cry to Thee
That Thy great Will may be fulfilled,
Thou answerest,
Thou answerest:
Beyond our utmost thought,
Swiftly and patiently, Thou answerest.

LORD,
In the hurry of everyday life, and of service for men,
We would snatch, again and again,
A hundred times a day,
The brief and golden leisure
To glance up to Thy face,
To catch once more the sound of Thy voice,
To feel anew the touch of Thy hand,
To know again that we live in Thee.

OUR souls are restless and fretful for Thee,
Thou Giver of rest and of peace;

As in a stifling night of the Rains
The air, lifeless and sultry,
Strangles and poisons with sickly fumes;
And he who would sleep
Wearily tosses from side to side
Desiring in vain one breath of coolness and peace:

Even so,
Our souls are faint for the breath of Thy coming,
Lying weary and sickened and choked
In the stifling night of the world:

Then come, ah come, and revive us,
Thou keen and glorious Wind,
Thou Spirit of the Living God.

WITHOUT Thee,
We are mariners wrecked in mid-ocean
Adrift on a wave-washed raft:
One by one we loosen our hold,
Fall back, and are swiftly engulfed.

Without Thee,
Like miners entombed
We wait in fevered despair,
Watching the water's remorseless rise, till we die.

Death has his hand on our throat,
Nought can save us at last from that sure close grasp,
His triumph draws steadily nigh.

Yet Thou, O our God,
Hast been through with it too:
Thou hast suffered the worst, and been strong:
Thou, too, hast been swept from the raft:
Thou, too, hast in agony waited and watched
As the slow waters rose inch by inch:
Thou, too, hast been stifled at last in the dark.

Be with us, our God,
Make us strong with Thy strength,
Unafraid at the last with Thy courage.

IN this white still moonlight,
Alone on the hill-top,
With the quiet forest around,
I pray Thee, O Father,
Make me Thy man
In truth and in deed:

Drive far from my soul
All sordid ambition,
All slackness in service of Thee:

Fill me with youth, with power, with joy,
That all I have, all I am
May be Thine.

FATHER,
Thy love is strong as the strength of the storm,
Resistless, unstaying, bearing all things before it:

Sweep through our narrow-souled lives this day,
With purity, fresh, keen, clear,
And with power:

Scourge us with Thy swift love,
That sloth, indifference, self,
May be rent from our lives:

That our hearts
May be filled, for ever,
With the tempest-breath of Thy love.

THY life, O God, beats through dull human hearts:
Thy life, Thy Spirit, works in men unceasingly,
Bidding them give themselves to Thee
In willing service of their fellows.

It is Thyself
Who strivest in dull human souls to right the wrong,
To lift the fallen and sustain the weak—
Thy Spirit burns in noble hearts, a steady flame of Will
beneficent,
Stalwart, unswerving, resolute
To heal and save Thy world.

Lord, live in us this day.
Even in us:
Lord, clothe Thyself, Thy purpose yet again
In human clay:
Work through our feebleness Thy strength,
Work through our meanness Thy nobility,
Work through our poverty of soul
Thy grace, Thy glory and Thy love.

O HOLY silence of our God,
When our souls, very joyfully forgetting
All the distractions and fretful cares,
All the hopes and the fears of earth,
Return to their home,
And are straightway at peace.

O holy and blessed silence,
When laying aside these petty and foolish lives,
We live in Him:
When our souls, deep drinking the joy of God's Heaven,
Put off age and decay,
Put on immortal and splendid youth,
Beauty incorruptible,
Life eternal.

O Father, grant us Thy grace,
That day by day, till our half-life on earth is over,
We may take from thy hands
This joyful and perfect sacrament of silence.

FROM this dark and fog-bound earth of ours
We take refuge in Thee once more,
O Rest of our souls,
Escaping, like birds from a broken cage,
To the keen clear air and the sunny uplands
Where Thou dwellest, and with Thee
Those who immortally live,
Blessed for ever in Thee,
Through their death here on earth.

From meanness of spirit,
From jealousy, slander, hypocrisy,
From selfish ambition,
From all the dank fumes that choke and strangle Thy Spirit
We take refuge in Thee.

Cleanse us, renew us, empower us,
By the living breath of Thy Heaven.

FOR Thy purpose of love and of power
Worked out in history
We thank Thee, our God, this day.

Teach us to love Thy human-kind
With a wide and comprehending love,
A love which faces the worst, and gives Thee thanks for the best.

Give us a passion to know,
To comprehend,
To drink in, with eager interest, the whole life-story
Of this Thy beautiful and marvellous creation,
Humanity,
Of this Thy handiwork, which Thou Thyself
Lovest eternally, passionately, comprehendingly,
Knowing the best and the worst,
Giving up with joy, for its sake,
Thine own immortal life.

FROM man's unfaithfulness
Our hearts turn longingly to Thee,
O Love eternal and unchanging.

From man's weak fickleness
Our hearts turn longingly to Thee
O Will immutable,

From man's small vapourings
Our hearts turn longingly to Thee,
O Word unspeakable.

From man's most sordid meanness
Our hearts turn longingly to Thee,
O Giver without stint or limit.

From man's exceeding feebleness
Our hearts turn longingly to Thee,
O Might omnipotent.

From man's gross filth
Our hearts turn longingly to Thee,
O Purity divine and absolute.

From man's deformity
Our hearts turn longingly to Thee,
O Beauty perfect and ineffable.

From man's dull hopelessness
Our hearts turn longingly to Thee,
O Hope immortal, and O deathless Joy.

Send us this day amongst our fellows,
Held every moment in Thine own strong friendship,
To be for Thee, triumphantly,
The heralds of Thy Will, Thy Word,
Thy generous Love, Thy Hope, Thy Joy,
Thy Might, Thy Purity, Thy Beauty.

TEACH us to-day,
O Master,
To rule ourselves,
To be stern, harsh, merciless
To our bodies and minds,
Teach us to rule our lives with an iron hand,
So that no sloth of ours,
No craven despair,
No base self-indulgence,
No failure of sympathy and imagination,
May mar the work of Thy Kingdom.

Teach us to-day,
O Master,
That true self-sacrifice
Which is yet a sacrament of joy,
Which never restrains the rich current of life
With narrow-souled, puritanical barriers,
But guides it with steadfast purpose,
Into one broad and generous channel—
The channel of that great Will of Thine,
Which is, for ever, abundance of life unto men.

WE hunger and thirst after Thee,
O Lover divine:

Our hearts are gaunt and shrivelled and parched,
Like a land sore smitten with famine:

O feed us to-day with this living food,
With Thyself:

May we drink in to-day Thy life,
Be transformed from weakness and sin
To the likeness of Thee.

CHRIST,
Teach us to-day
To pray, with Thee,
"Thy will be done":
Teach us Thy childlike confidence
In God's good care:
Teach us Thy fearless courage,

That, come what may—
Though the world be shattered around us,
Though life and joy go up in smoke,
Though naught be left but anguish and tears—
We may stumble forward, with Thee,
Unafraid, as Thou didst go to the Cross:

Teach us to trust continually
The rich unfailing love of the Father:

Teach us, O Christ, this day
Thy trust, Thy heart of strong courage.

MASTER,
Here in the pure white light of Thy dawn,
We pray for Thy whole wide world:

We pray for this little planet
Swingly thus swiftly around and around a lesser star,
One in a thousand million stars:

Yet for each several soul of the countless souls
That inhabit our planet,
Thou feelest, O King of all worlds, infinite passion of
love and pity and need—
More, unspeakably more,
Than a man can feel for his only child:

O Father of power and love,
Send forth on Thy world, and all in it,
The gentle might of Thy Spirit divine,
To show unto men Thy beauty,
To win them unto Thyself:

And for us we pray,
Make us Thy voice,
Thy tools.

CAPTAIN,
We pray Thee to-day for Thine own strong courage.

Give us courage to combat Thy enemies,
Give us courage to suffer in Thy cause:
Make us hard and remorseless towards ourselves:
Cleanse from our souls all futile sentiment:
Spur us this day to challenge the grim realities,
Pain, disease, injustice and sin,
And help us by gallant service to conquer these Thy

Give us wills alert and obedient,
Till we seek, not our own base ease,
But only the advancing of Thy Kingdom.

Toughen us, Master, by rigorous training and sternest use,
Till we are strong and hard as steel
In the doing of Thy great Will.

Yet keep us tender and kind as Thyself,
To all Thy little ones who need our service.

VII.

WORK

THEY have fled from their village,
She and her babes, to the forest;
Yet the pestilence slays them there too.

Naked she lies,
Beneath one torn blanket:
And her breath, harsh and reluctant,
Swift as a dog pants,
Comes feebler and fainter:
There is naught to be done for her now.

Close by her side sit the children,
Five years and three,
Wondering dully what it can mean,
And weeping a little,
For a week ago their father died too.

Lift up your eyes: and behold, close around,
The noonday splendour and shade of the forest:
The deep cool glades, and the golden sunlight:—
Beauty and grandeur and peace.

God, Maker of her and the forest,
Who lovest and yearnest for all Thou hast made,
Thou knowest and carest that thus untended sh
Show us, O God, Thy Will, and our duty, for these
die, and for Thee.

CHRIST,
Work in this flesh to-day,
Be manifest through us,
Reveal through us the love of God.

In Christlike word and thought,
In Christlike deed,
May these poor tongues and brains,
This mortal flesh we give to Thee,
Put on to-day a little of Thy likeness.

MASTER,
Here are our hearts and our souls this day,
Here is our deepest love,
Here is all the frail loyalty in us.
All the feeble and wavering will,
All the zeal, all the power of work, all the devotion:
Take Thou these gifts.

Poor gifts are they, and unworthy:
Yet, such as they are, they are Thine.

Take us to-day,
And rule us:
Keep us, ah keep us.
Close to Thyself.

Teach us to serve, in secret and humble ways,
Thy brethren, the needy and lost.

CHRIST,
For the men we pray
Before whom—in weakness and folly,
In emptiness, nothingness, shame—
We stand forth to-day, to tell them in word or in act of
Thyself.

Christ,
Send forth in their hearts.
The joyful might of Thy Spirit,
To show them Thy beauty,
To fill their souls with desire of Thyself.

Christ,
Hide *us*, hide *us*, Thy worthless and powerless tools,
And stand forth Thyself,
Calling Thine own, whom Thou lovest,
To high heroic achievement, to life for Thyself.

Christ,
May they see Thy beauty:
Christ,
May they fall in love with Thyself:
Christ,
May their souls be o'erwhelmed
With the deathless splendour of Thy free grace,
With yearning to live and to die for Thee,
To be held for ever by Thee,
Brethren, friends, of Thyself.

Christ,
Be manifest this day.

O GOD of youth, of joy, and of love,
Who madest the golden delight of the sunlit forest,
Who madest the craggy hills,
And the silvery bath of the moonlight,
Who gavest me eyes to behold this beauty,
Muscles to climb the crags, and to swim in the secret pools,

O God of beauty and love,
I thank Thee:

Teach me, oh teach me,
To live for Thee, and to show forth Thy beauty.

SET us to work this day,
O Thou who Livest,
Set us to work in joy, through loss of self:

Show us a need to meet,
Show us the meaning of our lives
In meeting of that need:

Lift, lift our eyes away, Christ Master, from ourselves,
And fix them wholly on Thy world without,
On beauty of Thy sun, Thy stars, Thy hills,
On grace and joy, love, courage, comradeship, in those around us,
As all revealing Thee, revealed to us in them by Thee.

CHRIST, Master,
God in a human life
Fully revealed:
To whom we look, and know
That God Himself is such
In love, in tenderness,
In courage, joyousness, humility,
And in simplicity:

Christ, Master,
Peasant, labouring-man,
Homeless, hungry wanderer,
Outcast: and—at the end—
Gibbetted criminal:

Christ, Master,
Brother, Saviour, Friend,
For ever living,
For ever strong to show us God:
God Thyself, in human flesh,
Perfect, complete:

Christ, Master,
Goal of our race in God,
Ideal final manhood
Whereto we strive,
Thyself the striving and the goal:

Lord Christ who diedst for us,
Who savest us,
Take us, use us, work through us, this day.

MASTER,
Thy goodness and grace are so rich in my life
I am shamed to the earth before Thee:

No return can I make Thee
For all Thou hast done:
Only a crippled and shaking will,
Only a fickle and wavering loyalty,
Only a heartless devotion,
Only a flickering glimmer of love:

Yet, Master, such as I am,
Such as I am, I give Thee myself—
Poor gift,
Sad, thankless task to make me a man,
To make me Thy man:

Yet, Master,
Take me:
For such as I am,
Here I am,
Given to Thee.

CHRIST,
Lover of fields and of flowers,
Lover of hills and of stars,
Lover of little children:

Christ, Teacher and Lord of the Open Air:

Christ, who didst come from the Open Air,
To be hounded to death in a stifling city
For Thy Kingdom of God:

Christ, Leader of all who would stand
For friendship and peace
Against hatred:

Christ, Hope—only Hope—of a world to be one hereafter:

Christ, who wast spat upon, crucified,
Because Thou wouldst sanction no hatred of race
against race:

Christ, who didst think, work, die,
For mankind as a whole:

Christ, who in each poor wreck of a man didst descry
embodied
Mankind as a whole, in its desperate need:

Christ, who in alien, outcaste, pagan, extortioner,
traitor,
Didst discern God's Light aflame,
God's child, to be won to the Father's home:

Christ, Captain,
Take Thou our lives, and live them to-day for Thy cause.

CHRIST,
Few and broken to-day
Are the words I can utter,
As thus, in the new white dawn Thou has given,
Adoring I kneel
To pour out my life—with all that I have and am—
Once more at Thy feet.

Few words and broken,
O Christ,
Are here in the stillness:
But what need of words?

Take me again,
Break the chain, ever renewed, of my weakness and shame,
Lift me up from the mire:

Take my will,
My power of love and of work
(Small, Thou knowest, it is):
Breathe through it Thine own iron will,
And use me this day.

O Christ,
Work through me to-day:
For I love Thee, a little at least:
And Thou
Art my All—
Art Truth and Beauty and Love
All summed in one Soul, that loveth *my* soul
For ever.

AFAR,
The silent dawn brightens beyond the forest,
And the whole wild world awakes into tingling joy:

Here,
Here in the city,
Men groan as they wake, as they wearily turn to their
work once more,
With hearts despairing, souls unrefreshed:

Grant, O Father, to us this day
Thy vision of joy from the forest:
That here, even here, in the pestilent city
We may carry with us the forest, the hills,
And go forth with courage and cheer to help in the work
of Thy Kingdom.

IDLENESS is rust and death,
But Work—hard, exhausting, rigorous labour,
Is God's good gift of life in action.

Save us then, Lord,
From this shameful disease of sloth,
From its living death.

Grant us the glory of Work,
Whose weariness is the crown of achievement,
Whose monotony is solid success,
Whose end is the end of a soldier,
Harness on back and face to the foe.

Use us, Lord, in Thy Work:
Use us remorselessly:
Grant us ever the guerdon of Work, of harder and sterner
Work.

Use us with pitiless rigour,
Wear us out for Thyself,
Till we pass from this feeble and stumbling activity
To full sharing at last in Thine own eternal Work.

IN the secret places of the hills,
The hidden glens, the narrow folded valleys—
Their grassy lawns bright-flecked with blossoms,
Their flanks fresh-sparkling with a thousand springs—
Remote from every dwelling-place of man,
With snow-crowned peaks above,—
There amidst the birches
In the secret of the hills
We may meet with Thee, our King:

There, there is Thy abiding-place,
There wilt Thou claim our souls
In mercy and in love, and with a deep and silent joy:

There, in the hidden valleys,
May we meet Thee,
And gain from Thy own hand
The strength for all our work.

FAR have we come to-day through the forest,
Crushed by the sun of May—
Even now, in the evening,
He scorches and shrivels and sears.

At the forest-hamlets the starving,
Gaunt, disease-stricken, naked,
Everywhere clamour around us,
Beseeching the aid—poor aid—that we bring.

Now at last, as the darkness falls,
Down-dropping from jungle-clad hills,
Where our guides go unwilling for fear of the tiger,
We reach Nágdon.

Black-dark are its narrow lanes;
For the night has fallen, sudden and swift.

We wearily stumble along, past the grass-built huts,
Each lit by its tiny and flickering wick.

At last we come down to our camp—
A mighty tree at the edge of the village;
Beyond it, the jungle again:
Beneath it, two cots and a crowd of the starving.

They have travelled from far, even cripples and blind,
When they heard of our coming:
All must be talked to and helped e'er we eat.

Then at last we may lie at our ease,
Gazing up through the leaves to the quiet stars
And sleep awhile, if the hot wind falls:
But at earliest dawn we must up and away.

VIII.

THE LOVE OF GOD

IN blue and misty moorlands,
In flowers starring the forest,
In shadowy lake-waters,
In snow-shrouded mountains on high,
In the fresh vivid green of the birches,
In sturdy pines that climb to the snow,
In keen tempestuous winds,
In racing clouds and glimpses of sun on lake and on forest—
In all this wealth of beauty and spring-time joy,
Thy glory, O God of the Open Air,
Is perfectly shown,
Thy love is revealed in might to our hungry souls

TRUE Heart that lovest me,
That gavest all for me, and givest still Thine all:
Brave Heart that diedst for me, for me,
And diest still:
Strong Heart, that sufferest Thine agony in man
Eternally:
Pure heart, that shrinkest not from all man's shame :—
O Christ, my King, my Friend,
O Christ, my God,
This day to Thee,
This day to Thee I give.

And, as forth I fare
Over the day's unseen expanse,
Following, feebly, stumblingly,
Thy guiding grace,
Held mightily by Thy heroic grace:
O Christ,
Be mine this glory and this joy to-day –
To show to one or two
Thy beauty and Thy love.

THE moonlight sleeps white on the forest,
The shadows are deep black pools,
A filmy shimmer of mist steals up from the silent lake:

For long leagues around, the forest, God's forest,
Breathes lightly, stirs gently, a living thing:

Ah God, dear God,
Known here so surely in moonlight, in forest, in silence,
God Who art King of it all,
Who livest and speakest so surely, so sweetly,
In the heart of it all:
God Who art Master of sun and of stars,
Yet Who lovest this weak little creature, myself, this
timid and narrow soul:
God, dear God of the Open Air,
Hallow my life, make it white, make it silent save in
Thy praise,
As is this fair forest moonlight.

NO words are there to be found, for ever,
For the things that truly exist,
Nothing but fruitless gropings after expression.

No words are there to thank God for the joy He has given,
No words to set forth His splendour,
No words to speak of this fair revelation of Him
In the wonderful world He has made, and in sweet human love.

Here in the silence of evening,
Our souls wide-opened to Heaven,
We will kneel, and pray for His grace,
That, where words are foolish and meaningless,
Our lives may speak of His love.

FATHER,
No glimpse of light can we see
On our future path:
But our hands are held, by Thy mighty hand:
And Thou canst see.

Therefore, fearless and unafraid,
We will march through the darkness,
Upheld and guarded and led by Thy love,
Well knowing that every step of the way
Shall prove Thee more faithful and tender,
More wholly enough for all that we need.

O Father,
Our hearts and our lives, with deep and secret delight
We render to Thee:
And forward we press, on our great adventure
Of this day Thou hast given,
To discover still wider and fairer realms
Of Thy great love,
And to labour for Thee.

HERE, on the wide and desolate moorland,
Alone in the silvery moonlight,
And afar from the dwellings of men,
We will worship the King.

The day, with its tyrannous heats, is behind us,
The glare of the sunlight is gone:
The Indian night, in its magical beauty,
Has granted us coolness and peace.

O Master and Friend,
Who makest it all, Who indwellest it all,
Whose splendour and power divine
Are revealed in it all.

Who lovest our souls, as a mother her child,
Yet a thousand times more,
Take this service of peace and delight,
Take the happy thanks of our hearts.

O THOU great Lover of our race,
Thou who hast led us upward from the beast,
Thou who in blood and mire, in conflict and in agony,
Hast struggled ceaselessly, in man for man:

O Thou who sufferest when we suffer,
Thou who in human strife and hatred
Art crucified again,
Thou who art slain a thousand thousand times
That man may live:

O Thou who dwellest very close to each of us,
Very close to every man in every age:
O Thou without whose presence
We perish in the night,
In this one heart at least
Establish Thou Thy victory to-day.

POOR and weak and worthless is my heart,
Stained by sin, harassed by self-love;
Yet here, even here—ah wonder beyond word and thought—
Here doth He come to abide.

Ruler is He of all worlds,
Reigning supreme over stars and suns:
Over forest and ocean and hill
He holdeth His dominion absolute:
He may choose His abode where He will.

Yet not afar doth my King choose it,
In the glory of the starlit silent heavens:
He chooseth it not afar,
In the splendour of snow-veiled mountain or the shadowy depths of the forest.

But here, here in this heart, restless and fickle and stained—
Ah love beyond belief—
Here in this heart He abideth with me, even with me.

OUR souls would be silent this morning,
O Father and Lover and Friend,
To learn from Thyself,
Through the silent touch of Thy love,
Thy will for our lives and the lives around us:

Our souls would be silent,
To drink, in the silent dawn,
Deep from the springs of Thy peace.

Teach us, we pray,
To be silent before Thee:
Give us a teachable spirit:

Day after day
Reveal to us, ever more silently, surely and deeply,
Thy love, and Thy will for this needy world.

O SAVIOUR, Sustainer, Friend,
Thus to meet Thee again, in another new day,
Is heaven indeed.

Through the darkness and stupor of night,
Thou hast been with us each moment—
Full well do we know it:
Yet thus to awake, and to feel Thy presence,
To know thus afresh the thrill of Thy strength round our weakness.
To look up to Thy face,
To catch thus its smile of courage and love,
To see, before us,
A new golden day with Thyself,
To know that Thou, who lovest each creature on earth,
Lovest us, even us, who in weakness kneel here,
With Thy whole divine heart
Just for our own individual selves—
This, ah this,
Is heaven indeed.

SO little and weak am I,
O Father:
So great and so strong art Thou:
Yet Thou lovest me,
Thou lovest even me,
Even me, with all my folly and sin,
For myself Thou lovest:

Even in me, in me,
O Father and Lover divine,
Thou canst see, canst feel,
Something that calleth forth, even to death,
Thine eternal love, and fixeth it firm,
In all its power and fulness,
Upon me, even on me.

O Father, Father,
I thank Thee:
With all my puny irresolute nature
I love Thee, desire to be Thine,
Yearn to give back unto Thee
Something of all that I owe,
Ache with heart-felt longing to serve Thee, to work
for Thy Kingdom:

Father,
Dear glorious Father,
I love Thee.

AS, long ago, Thy quiet voice,
O Christ,
Gave on the lake calm after storm:
So also now, in this sweet silent morning hour,
Still with Thine own authority
All busy clamorous voices of the world.

A hundred little plans we have to make,
A hundred little cares of foolish zeal
Beset our souls:
Still, still these loud insistent sounds
That deafen all our life with importunity,
With trivial hateful claims.

Settle our souls in silence at Thy feet,
That thus at last,
(The clamour dying swiftly, and Thy peace
Flooding our spirit with its healing grace)
Life may come back to us; our souls
May waken, open wide their eyes,
And see Thy face bent over us in love,
And feel Thy hand upraising us,
And know again our home.

AROUND us is infinity,
And we are nothing.

Star beyond star:
Universe beyond universe,
Unending for ever:

A million years to the making of man,
A thousand million to the making of the rocks:
We are beset, this side and that side, by eternity:

Yet what of it all,
This infinite space, this endless time?
Kings are we of it all,
For, O King of it all, we love Thee, Who art Love:
And our hearts are at rest in Thyself
Who art more than it all,
In Whom all time, all space, are summed up,
One radiant thought of Thy mind,
One urge of Thy love, one pulse of Thy life,
That life which even through us
Triumphantly beats, destroying death and necessity.

IX.

FRIENDSHIP

HERE, in the forest-dawn,
Whilst around me is wrought
Thy miracle,
Lord,
Of a new-born day:
Here, 'midst the quiet trees,
Where nought is heard save the drowsy note of a wakening bird:
Here, in the holy silence and strength of dawn
Alone on the hill-top,
I render my soul unto Thee,
O my God.

Brief is man's life,
Set between darkness and darkness
Yet long enough is man's life to know Thee,
O generous-hearted,
O tender-hearted,
O loyal and loving God.

Here, in the silence of dawn,
I worship, I drink in Thy life,
Dear, great-hearted Father and Friend,
Who canst love even me:

Make me Thy man,
And use me to-day for Thy Kingdom.

DEEP and silent and cool as a broad still tree-
shadowed river
Is the peace of Thy presence, Thou Rest of our souls.

From the thousand problems of this our hurrying life
We turn, with silent joy, to plunge in Thee,
To steep our souls in Thy quiet depths,
Where no clamour of earth disturbs our perfect content.

Thou art our Home and our Refuge;
In Thee we are safe and at peace:
Ever, in the din and hurry of the world
We know that Thou art near,
We know that close at hand—closer far than our own
little life—
Floweth that silent river of Thy presence and Thy love.

In a moment we may be with Thee and in Thee,
In a moment be surrounded and soaked in Thy peace:
In a moment, as this loud world clangs around us,
We may rest secure in the bliss of Thine eternity.

EAST and West men strive for their rights,
Men hunger for freedom:

Yet Thou, O Friend divine, art in truth the only freedom
for man,
The only right, inalienable, of each human soul,
The only loyalty for all mankind,
The one home-land.

TEACH us, O Christ, this day
Thy greatest lesson,
To love our fellow-men,
To love them purely
With no least taint of selfishness,
No jealousy,
No greed,
No rivalry,
No lurking itch for recognition:

Teach us Thy greatest lesson,
Pure, joyful, Christlike friendship.

THEY tell us of systems and rites,
Of schemes of redemption, philosophies, dogmas, and creeds;

But how can faith deal with dead things
In a world where are mountains and forests and stars,
Children's laughter and love, and the touch of God's hand?

Faith is vivid and living and warm,
Faith is friendship with Thee.

Not from books and authority, pedants or priests,
Cometh faith, but from life lived with Thee,
O Master divine,
From the joy of the friendship of God.

O THOU, who art, beyond all human telling,
Beautiful, adorable and lovely:
Thou who revivest our souls,
Thou who fillest our lives with joy,
Thou whose touch on our hearts is bliss, deathless and ineffable,
Thou at whose word of love monotony, grief and despair flee away,
Thou who makest the desert a garden with Thy presence,
Thou with whom to live, in humble poverty and weakness,
Is splendour of eternal life,
Give us this day the light and glory and joy
Of Thy perfect Friendship.

AT darkest midnight,
When the furnace breath of the hot-weather storm-blast shivers the parched up leaves,
When the body is wearied and fevered
And the mind distraught,
When sleep is afar,
When each tiny sound
Is a needle to stab me awake,
When the cares and the faults of the day
Are magnified thousand-fold,
When I toss to and fro
And yearn for the dawn,
Yet yearn even more
For coolness and darkness and sleep:

In that dreadful hour of night
Suddenly there shall be Peace:
A Presence divine shall be with me,
The sound of a Voice,
The touch of a cooling hand:
And stilled by Thee, O my Lover, my God,
I shall sleep:

For wherever my need is greatest,
There art Thou nearest, O Friend, to help and to save.

HARD and lonely at first is the path of duty,
With deep desolation of spirit,
With stagnation and darkness of mind,
With continuing weariness of body.

Then, dim through the blackness of night,
A Light shall be seen,
Whose feeble beams shall slowly expand
To a new, unguessed-at radiance of joy.

At last
He that despaired shall know Thy presence, O God,
Shall know that, having Thee,
He has all things needful and goodly, in generous measure.

For in following duty is gained the fulness of life,
And loneliness leads to the Friendship divine.

TEACH me, O Christ,
Thy full humility;

May I rejoice that my friends are better than I,
May I seek, and find, some lowly and humble service,
Obscure and remote.
And there may I lose myself in the need of the men around me.

Teach me, O Christ,
Thy full simplicity:

May I be glad in the gifts Thou hast given,
Desiring no more:
May I deny myself:
May I believe in men,
Till by power of faith in their better selves
I help to make them what Thou wouldst have them to be.

Teach me, O Christ, these Thy great lessons, and hard:
Thine own humility,
Thine own simplicity.

NOT alone in the darkness of grief do we need Thee,
Not alone in the splendour of joy,
Not alone in the wild open-air would we thrill to Thy presence,
Not there alone would we know ourselves Thine;

But here in the dull monotonous round,
Here in the steady rhythm of everyday work
Here where so little uplifts and so much degrades and
oppresses,
Here above all do we need Thee, our God.

Here above all be our Rock and our Fortress,
Silent and strong in the heart of the hurry and strife:
Here in the clamour vouchsafe us the grace of Thy
presence,
Here in the darkness and gloom enkindle our hearts by
Thy touch.

YESTERDAY,
Pursuing a passing motor in the street—
A thing I have often forbidden and punished—
My dog fell, by evil chance,
Beneath a cart, and his leg was crushed into splinters.

I carried him straight to the doctor,
Who stretched him out on a table,
Pulled out the shattered leg to its proper place,
And kneaded the splinters into position.

He bore the fierce pain like a hero,
With never a cry or a struggle:
Only, with great trustful eyes,
He gazed up at me, his master,
As I stood by his side, with my hand on his head.

Even so also, O Master Divine,
When my own time comes,
May I bear my pain like a hero,
Caring only that Thou standest there
Bearing it all at my side.

AT earliest dawn,
With the moon's thin sickle adrift on high, through the undimmed stars,
And the birds' first murmuring notes as yet unheard—
At earliest dawn,
Whose woolly head do I spy,
Raised from his pillow and wreathed in a broadening smile
As he sees I am there?

Thank God for another day, thus begun,
Of jolliest friendship with thee, little son:
Thank God for another day
Of riotous baby-laughter,
Of a house re-echoing cries of delight,
Of heaven-born beauty, simplicity, grace,
Lent us to learn from and love, here in our home.

Thank God for another day of thy life,
Small son,
Whose few brief months have taught us so much
Of God and God's love.

STRONG Friend,
Who walkest with me every road, unseen,
Sustaining patiently my tottering steps,
Breathing Thy courage to my coward heart,
Joy beyond joy bestowing, all unmerited:

Comrade, Leader, King:

Teach me to live beyond myself this day,
To hope, and pray, and work
Wholly for others:

Save me, oh save me, Living Christ,
From all self-pity,
From jealousy,
From self-advertisement;
For these are death and hell:

Fling forth my life upon the world,
In every thought and deed,
Victoriously self-transcending.

HEART of love,
Close beating here by our own:
Heart so human, so familiar,
So comprehensible to those that love:

Heart of rest and comfort
Heart where our spirits are at home
In sweet serenity and peace:

Heart of our most tender and most loving God,
Whose might omnipotent controls the stars,
Whose will unchanging sways the Universe.
(Yet what are these high-sounding attributes
Beside this only, that Thou lov'st our souls,
Lov'st even us?):

Ah! heart belovéd and divine,
Sustain us, all this day,
With Thy great love.

X.

THE SACRAMENT OF NATURE

HERE in the stifling heat, and in thronging pressure of work,
I thank Thee, my God,
That out and beyond, in the wild,
There is coolness and peace:

May I bear in my heart, untouched by the world,
Through labour, anxiety, pain,
Through heat and the harassing follies of everyday work,
The great silent hills, and the murmuring forests.

FATHER,
For all this beauty and strength of the sea,
For white-capped billows, flashing afar,
For the gleam of the myriad sun-kissed facets on each long roller,
For the wild free joy of the sea-birds,
For fresh keen wind, our brother,
For the hazy horizon,
Dimly opening up, hour after hour, before us,
As our good ship drives her way onward,
Ever disclosing fresh vistas of cloud and of shadowy waters—
For all this beauty and strength of Thy sea,
Thy name, O our Father, be praised, be mightily praised.

HERE e'er the first dull glow of the dawn
Has enkindled the east,
We worship before Thee, O Father;

Here e'er the slow-wheeling stars are dimmed
Our spirits are gathered and bowed before Thee,
Our life with its ill-spent years of the past,
Its faculties dwarfed, misused,
All its stunted powers of love and of speech for Thee,
Is summoned and grasped in a gathering-point
Of fierce expectation:

Beneath this vast, glittering throne of Thy glory,
The star-swept heavens,
We wait:

Around us the dawn-wind begins its faint breathing:

We wait,
Marshalling silent before Thee,
Our life, as a shepherd marshalls his flock:

Ah, Thou art here,
We lift up our eyes, and we see;
We lift up our hearts, and we know:

Ah God, Thy Love,
Simple, intimate, lowly—:

Thou, Lord of all worlds,
Enter our dreary souls,
And make us Thine own.

STRAIGHT and deliberate falls the rain,
The plane-trees are clad, at last,
In their gauzy veil of fresh buds,
The soft expanse of the valley is dim and shrouded
beneath us:

Above, the pine-woods climb.
Sturdy, unwearied, up to the snow:

O Father, as evening comes down on this beauty and joy,
We bring Thee, here in the dreamy twilight,
Our lives once more:
Make Thou this beauty and joy, this infinite peace,
Part of ourselves,
May we live in it all our lives, and in Thee who art Sum
and Source of it all.

FOR Thy mountains, O Father,
We thank Thee this day:

For Thy deep-cut valleys,
Filled with Thy solemn music of turbulent waters:

For Thy forests hanging above,
With their stately and ancient trees:

For Thy crags that jut from the forests,
Shattered and thunder-riven:

For Thy long, bright grass-slopes above the crags,
Thick strown with the glory of flowers,
Where the swift mountain-goat and the surly bear have
their home,
And a few gnarled trees march stalwartly upwards:

Then for Thy snow we thank Thee,
Thin scattered at first,
And above, fathomless, frozen, ablaze in Thy sunshine:

But for Thy peaks, O Father,
How shall we thank Thee?
Those pinnacles, steely, remote, dwelling aloof in
another world,
The goal of our long endeavour,
Where our souls can meet Thee,
Can speak with Thee face unto face . .

For the throne of Thy ultimate splendour,
Thy great mountain peaks,
How shall we thank Thee, our God?

A SKY deep-dyed with the purple of night,
Clouds tinged with orange,
And a great wide splendid full-moon
Sailing in majesty over the heaven
Attended and decked by a feathery halo of cloud:

Ambrosial night,
Warm, flower-scented, instinct with beauty and laughter:

Stamp, O our God, on our souls
The meaning, the truth of it all—
Of Thy dazzling ineffable beauty:

And send us forth,
To spread in darksome and pestilent places
This beauty, this truth.

NOT salt sea water,
But liquid azure,
Blue in its inmost being, with a deep irridescence,
Numbing the mind with its blueness,
Surpassing all word, all expression, all thought:

Each tiny ripple
Poised on the crest of a long blue billow,
Or deep in the hollow beneath,
Is blue itself, with a blueness ethereal, passing belief:

And the sky overhead,
More liquid still than the sea beneath,
More wondrously tinted in depth and translucence of
azure:

For this Thy Mediterranean sea,
O Christ, who didst live on its shores,
For its dazzling blueness, its beauty beyond all telling,
Thy name we praise and adore.

SOFT falls the rain on the river,
A thousand pattering drops, with their tiny rings,
That spread, and are mingled, and lost.

Low on the hills the great clouds brood,
Hiding all but the lowest bastions
With a curtain, restful and dim,
Whereunder they sleep.

Swift and silent the river
Hurries, with blind irresistible impulse
To its home in the sea,
As the soul of man yearningly hastens
Home unto God.

STEEL-GREY lies the lake;
Over its dreamy waters a wandering breeze,
Slow-passing, sways gently the reeds by the shore,
And dims the translucent reflection
Of tree and crag and the shadowy mountains.

On high, a broad girdle of fleeciest cloud
Encircles the snow-peak;
Through it the highest pines
Once and again are faintly discerned,
Swathed in its ghost-like vapours;
Above it the snow-fields gleam,
Virgin-white, inviolate.

Southward, far o'er the vale,
Blue hills are faint to be seen
Through the bands of rain which the soft west wind
Drifts gently before it.

Thus night falls, holy and calm,
Instinct with the stillness of God.

Slowly, from over the darkening waters,
An eagle wings its way home to the crag,
As a soul that wings its way home
To the safety and strength of God.

ACROSS the silent lake, deep-shadowed,
The giant tempest-clouds sweep up,
Deep living purple, with the lightning-flash
Quick and ecstatic in their gloomy bosom:

Soon God's good gift of rain,
In solid ceaseless mass,
Will blot the world from sight, from sound, from knowledge,
In one impenetrable, viewless torrent:

O Father, Who in quiet lake and clamant storm
Indwellest mightily and lovingly Thy world,
Dwell also, with Thy power and majesty and love,
In this dull heart of mine.

FATHER, we thank Thee to-day for the forest:
For feathery grasses, red-gold in the splendour of sunset,
For the call of the birds,
For the whisper of forest-life all round,
For winding paths that are lost ahead in the shadows,
For the trees, tall silent fountains of beauty and light,
For the lake below,
The lake that by day is a burnished glory,
And by night a mirror of star-flecked eternity,
Gazing wherein our spirits break loose from the bonds of time and of death,
Knowing their End in Thyself:

For all this sacred, mysterious beauty,
Sacrament unto our souls of Thy life divine,
We thank Thee, our Father, we thank Thee, this day.

FOR lake-water, Father,
I thank Thee to-day:

Here swimming far from the shore,
My being held and enwrapped
In this warm and gracious caress,
I thank Thee, O Father:

Overhead are the birds,
Wheeling and flashing in lissom delight,
And the sunset-clouds, kindled to vividest scarlet,
As the sky flames forth its salute to the parting day:

By my side darts hither and thither,
Even so far from the shore,
In swiftest diagonal flight,
A dragon-fly, splendid in green and in gold:

The trees stand knee-deep in the flooded waters,
They wade out from the hill to rejoice in such brimming
wealth:

All this generous open-air world
Is aflame and ashout with Thy goodness, O God.

PENT here in the city, walled round by houses,
Dwelling all day within narrow bounds,
How shall I find Him, the Lord of the open air?

Yet, remember: beyond there is the forest,
League after league of coolness and of silence,
League after league of the beauty He has made.

Then come the hills, His hills,
Blue against the sunset, bewitched beneath the moon-
light,
Transfigured in the dawn.

Aye, I will remember
The forest and the mountains,
The great open spaces,
The wind in the trees, and the lonely hill-tops.

ABROAD, on a star-lit night,
With the empty moors around,
And the night-wind softly blowing,
There is Thy palace, O King.

There in the peace and the beauty of night,
With the silence around,
And the flaming heavens above,
There is Thy palace, O King.

There may our souls know Thee,
Know Thee and worship Thy might,
Rejoice in the touch of Thy love:
There is Thy palace, O King.

FOR sunset over the lake,
I thank Thee, O Father;
For dark bands of cloud,
And the golden splendour behind them:
For crisp waves racing before the wind,
For the joyful call of the birds,
For the wideness and peace of the sky,
For the shadow and shine on the water,
As night falls fast,
For the surge of the gale in the trees:

For all this beauty and joy,
The gift of Thy grace,
I thank Thee, O Father.

CLEAR lake-water, thick-studded with starry
blossoms:
Far snow-summits, washed by the billowy clouds:
A keen west wind, and racing waves,
That toss our canoe as she shears through the lotus-beds:
Rain-belts sweeping afar and hiding the upland pastures
Where in shaggy bands the wild hill-ponies play:

Ah God, how fair is Thy world,
And how close and joyful and dear
The great warm heart of Thy love.

THE night falls swift as we splash through the ford,
And, breasting the slope beyond,
Come at last to the camping-ground:

A few low huts, where the famine-folk dwell,
The river wandering by, with its silent pools,
And the murmur of rapids afar:

Around, the desolate plains,
Not a tree breaks their barren expanse:
On the farthest horizon dim hills lift their heads through
the dust-haze:

The sky, so cruel and blasting by day,
Soft-lighted now in the evening, quiet and mild,
Shows us the twinkling points of the new-born stars:

In the West, a dull furnace-glow,
Where the Enemy, wearied at last,
Sank even now to his rest.

Here will we stay through the stifling night:
We shall sleep in the open,
The stars for our tent:

But first we will swim together,
A long cool swim,
In the river-pool by the ford,
While the night-bird whistles and calls overhead,
And the fire-flies glimmer and dance in the reeds,
And God gives coolness at last and peace to our souls.

AGAIN, O King of our lives,
We worship, whilst yet it is night, at Thy feet:

Above, rides the moon, the thinnest of sickles,
And beside her two great and radiant stars
Hang, like silvery lamps:

In the East the first red tinge of the coming day
Is kindling the low-lying clouds to fire:

O wonder ever renewed of Thy power, our God,
Creating beauty and life,
Dispelling darkness by light divine:

In this silent, mysterious dawn,
Very closely art Thou to be known:

Disguise and convention stripped clear,
Open we stand and plain to Thy sight,
Worthless, unable to please Thee,
Unable to worship or praise:

Yet crowned with ineffable glory,
Kings of the world, lords of all ages,
Since Thou, the infinite God,
Lovest us,
Longest for us, and yearnest—O miracle passing belief—
Yearnest for our poor love.

Vijayanagar

FOREST-CLAD hills around
And the murmuring river below:

Here, on a rock-strewn space between river and hills,
Remote and desolate,
Fast mouldering to dust,
The ruined city:—

Once, an abode of kings,
Mistress of a far-flung empire,
Filled with the thronging traffic of three broad continents:

Now, silent, tenantless,
Sleeping unseen, unknown,
Between the river and the hills.
Assailed at all points by the conquering forest:

But very lovely is she still, this City of Forgotten Victory:
Temple and palace,
Richest profusion of tall sculptured columns,
Long silent streets, here in the heart of the forest:

After life's fierce and passionate dream
The Soul of the City rests,
Content, in the wild forest beauty.

THE Western sky is aflame with the sunset,
Black clouds above,
Deep pools of red and orange and gold on the sky-line:
And afar, on a long dark ridge,
Soaring aloft, stalwart and stark,
Sharp-cut on that radiant sky,
A single pine-tree:

Seen from near by that tree will be black and obscure,
Undistinguished, as night comes down, from its fellows:
But thus descried, five miles away, and in front of the
sunset,
It stands sublime.
Stately and lonely and splendid,
Pointing the way to heaven:

So also, O Master, may our lives be:
Undistinguished here from our fellows,
Obscure, unassuming and humble:
But seen from afar,
Over the long dark waste of the years,
May they stand forth clear and splendid for Thee,
Illumined, aflame, in the fire divine
Of Thy great love,
Pointing the way unto Thee.

TO force your way up crags that have never been climbed before;
To run out ninety feet of rope
On the sheer cold face of the cliff
Before a belay can be found, and the rope secured
For the next man to follow:
To reach a perilous cranny, beyond a lip of the rocks,
Where you stand alone on the toppling crags,
With nought below but blue air,
And nought above but the bastions of the peaks,
And nought of human companionship
Save the thin down-trending rope:

To gain, after hours of strenuous leadership,
The airy ultimate summit,
And to look forth thence, true monarch of all you can see,
Upon mountain and valley and lake:
This, this, is to quaff
In long deep draughts
The rich red wine of life.

THE silent forest singeth aloud to His name,
Bird and flower, the noonday blaze and the dim-lit
evening,
He liveth in all, and in the glory of all He is praised.

O world most beautiful, most secret and most holy,
World of the open-air, of moorland and snow-crowned
mountain,
Of wide-bosomed heavens and flame-fingered dawn:

O world of His living presence, world of the knowledge
of God—
Knowledge divine, that is neither of sect, nor of creed,
nor of rite,
Knowledge divine, that is living and sure and ineffably
sweet.

O beautiful world, world beyond telling most lovely,
Alone in the dawn, on this wind-washed hill-summit,
I kneel and adore.

MILE after mile of mysterious woodland,
Where the monkeys play and the peacocks call:
Mile after mile of coolness and beauty and peace
Till the heart is drugged with delight:
Mile after mile of soft clouds overhead,
Of bands of rain on the forest,
Of sweet-scented breeze in our faces.

Long curving ascents, at the top
A gap in the forest-wall,
And through it a vista, far seen,
Of deep-bosomed hills, splashed here and there with the
sunlight,
Of winding rivers that gleam in the valleys,
Of tiny green fields by the forest-girt hamlets:
A goodly land, and a fair,
This land of Seoni.

The Tent-door

THROUGH the wild and exultant flame of our fire
Is fitfully seen the high black wall of the mountain,
Its edge pine-fringed,
Its summit a steely point on the stars:

Beneath, the snow-swollen torrents roar
Rending the night with their solemn thunder:

Around us, the sombre pine-stems
Are dyed to a dull red glow in the flames,
And afar, through the long-fingered branches,
The high snows gleam.

An owl hoots sudden o'erhead:
From far up the cliff an answer returns.

The night is awake, the darkness ablaze,
With the presence and splendour of God.

NAUGHT but the song of a lark—
Yet its cadence holds hidden
The power of God.

For it breaks, with a sure and effortless might,
The brazen fetters of time and of space,
And it flings my soul forth,
Like a bird set loose from its cage,
On the free keen winds of eternity—
The winds that sweep me away to that land
Where are sights and sounds,
Joy and beauty and peace,
Ne'er to be spoken by human tongue.

ACROSS the broad-bosomed lake
Steadily blows the brave west wind,
Damp and cool and delicious,
Scented with blossoms afar,
For the Rains are with us at last.

The clouds, huge toppling galleons, radiant-sailed,
One close-chasing another, in silent and stately array,
Swiftly fare through the billowy sea of the wind-swept heavens.

The waves on the shore
Plash with a musical call:
Behind on the tree-tops the birds
In a chattering conclave gather their ranks for the night.

The frogs in the reeds
Already are tuning their rollicking chorus:
And all of this forest-world is gleeful and blest
In coolness and moisture and life
After scorching and shrivelling death.

So into the flashing delight of the water
We slip for a long lazy swim,
As beneficent darkness falls,
And the last golden sheen of the sunset dies on the ripples.

AN ice-cold wind
That whips great flakes from the cornice
And sends them spinning
With a tinkling clang, like a fairy bell,
Down the sheer snow-slope to the north.

Around, a world of snow,
Pierced, near at hand, by a few dark rocks,
The arête we have climbed:
A long black line it stretches below—
Then a gap for the crags we scaled:
Beyond, the eye may follow it down, our arête,
Till it merges at last, a dizzy distance below,
With the long steep ridge,
Where the grass and the juniper struggle for life,
Brown wisps through the covering white.

So down in successive descents,
Downward the long ridge falls,
Through the feathery birch,
White-stemmed, gnarled and twisted by tempests,
Ever the nearest of trees to the snow,
Past the radiant gentian-beds,
To the pines at last,
To the pointed pines:
Tiny they seem, those pines,
In the deep blue gulf of air:
Yet each a two-hundred foot giant:

Upward they climb, the pines,
Four thousand feet, from the valley,
Where, hard by the grey Liddar-stream,
The stern-voiced, ice-fed Liddar,
Our little encampment stands.

On our own ethereal level, our neighbours,
The snow-veiled, rock-ridged peaks,
Dream in the silence.

Yet it is not utterly silent,
This world of the snows;
For hark, that distant thunderous roar
Is an avalanche, crashing its way resistless
From yon great peak, down its dizzy flanks,
To the forest below,
Whirling the pines in ruin.

O God of this marvellous world of the mountains,
On this airy ultimate throne of Thy glory,
Washed with this lustral profusion of golden light,
We give Thee the praise of our hearts.

Father, our Father,
Who madest it all, art revealed in it all,
In Whom alone we have life, and eyes to behold Thy
    glory,
Small and remote on this ultimate summit
We give Thee the praise of our hearts.

Taxila

BARE hills around
Darkening fast as the evening falls:

Here in the valley,
With the stream softly calling below,
A few ruined walls—
A palace once—
Deserted, silent, mouldering to dust:
An ancient stairway, dinted deep,
Some scattered fragments of mosaic,
And a broken shrine.

That is all.

Yet turn not hence disdainfully away,
For these poor shattered halls
Were once gay-decked
To welcome the all-conquering Macedonian:
These crumbling stones
Were trodden by those wingéd feet,
And on these brooding hills
Once gazed the eyes of Alexander.

BITTER cold, freezing a man's very life,
Dark rocks around,
And above a few steely stars:
One querulous note of a half-wakened bird,
Faint heard from the forest below,
And the breath of a wind chill as death.

Then,
By the sudden stroke of the finger of God,
To the East a red glow,
And against it, faint-seen,
The keen saw-edge of the giant Himálaya,
Black, desolate, and terrible.

To the West, a dimness,
A glow,
A flame,
A splendour of molten gold,
As Everest takes the dawn.

Soon,
East to West,
The northward horizon, from end to end,
Shines with a glory of rose-crested peaks,
The mightiest in the world—

Thus God is revealed once again.

FATHER,
The beauty of Thy world, in sunshine and rain-shadow,
Singeth aloud of Thy love:
Each tint of the autumn leaves,
Each breath of the keen west wind,
Each flower, each bird,
Each glimpse of the sun through the clouds,
Lighting the woods and the hills afar,
Is a sight of Thy face,
Thy face of beauty and love.

THE night falls fast.

Ahead shines a radiant sunset,
Clouds black-dark,
Through them swift-thrusting, lances of roseate light:
Beyond, where the long blue hills have caught and hidden the Sun,
Faint-seen banners of gold and scarlet,
Dipping and rising afar, as in some great fight.

In the valley resounds, through the silence of twilight,
The steady and sonorous roar of the cataract:
The lake is still as a mirror, a molten ocean of gold.

All things are filled with a beauty divine, surpassing speech or belief,
Instinct with the presence of God.

HERE in the dim mysterious forest,
Sit we silent an hour,
And live.

At first, our minds wander afar:
The call of the wood-dove,
The sonorous hum of the insects,
The merry clamour of parrots,
The sough of the wind in the trees,
Like the steady beating of waves on a rock-bound coast:
All the thousand voices of forest-life
Entice us afield and away.

But soon,
The spell of the forest-silence falls on our spirit,
And in long deep draughts
We drink in its benediction,
And live.

We become,
Not these diverse creatures of body and mind,
Of fickle impulse and fevered activity,
But living souls in the living world
Of the Living God.

We put off death,
We put on life,
We behold the Truth:

In bliss beyond words
Our souls are joined unto Him,
And in Him to each other.

ABOVE, three hundred feet of sheer rock-wall,
Festooned with a feathery network of fern,
And moist with the silvery rain from a hundred springs.

Beneath, the deep still green of the water,
Unfathomed, dark-shadowed,
Divinely cool.

The ramparts, here where we swim, but six feet sundered:
And on high but a narrow ribbon of fervent light
To show where the midsummer noonday sears and blinds.

Behind and before, nought to be seen but the curving walls of the cleft,
And the dreamy waters winding into the shadows:
Nought to be heard but the myriad drip from the walls.

Slowly we breast the water,
Despatching far in advance, a lazy ripple,
That gently caresses the fern-fronds on either side.

CLEAR is the dawn upon the mountains;
Far below, in the mist-shrouded valley,
An eagle, slow-circling alone in effortless flight,
Steadily cleaves his way with majestic power,
Through the blue, empty air.

Faint, from five thousand feet down,
Rises the roar of the snow-swollen torrent:
And above are the steely peaks.

Here in mid-heaven,
With the flanks of the mountains steeply falling below,
And the snow close above,
We may rest for a moment and know.

We may know the heart of it all,
Feel through it all the beat of the life divine,
Thrill with the knowledge of God
In the beauty and splendour of mountain-dawn.

We may ache, a little as He too aches,
With desire that empty and broken and joyless lives,
In all His world,
May be free, may rejoice, and may know.

BROAD and strong flows the river to the sea:
A week ago there was nought but sand and glare in her mighty bed,
With a thin little brook in the midst, daily shrinking away.

But the Rains came in their might;
For a thousand miles every hill, rejoicing in freshness and leafage,
Sent down to the river its numberless streams.

And now, fifty feet deep, half-a-mile wide,
Banks far overflowed,
The Mother exults in her strength.

Silent is she in her strength,
No thunderous roar comes up to the ear:
To the eye there is nought but a level expanse of quick-gliding waters,
Racing past and away, swifter far than a man may run on her bank,
Whirling here the trunk of a stalwart tree,
There the roof of a house,
Relentless in steady determined power.

Even so is the Will of God.
Deep and broad, silent, swift and omnipotent.

XI.

SALVATION

N

AH, agony divine
Of Thy great Heart, our God,
When all Thy world is wandering far from Thee,
Rent by wild faction,
Filth-begrimed with selfishness and greed,
Alight, fierce-blazing in the glare of sin:—

Ah, agony eternal of Thy heart divine,
To see the men Thou lovest
Thus squander heedlessly the perfect joy,
The grace and purity and life which Thou wouldst give:—

Ah, agony eternal of Thy heart divine,
That men will break from Thee, who diedst for them,
Who livest endlessly for them,
Will break from Thee, rejecting Thy strong love,
To waste in shame the manhood Thou hast given.

CHRIST,
God-revealer to mankind, eternally,
Thyself eternal God, most perfectly revealed:

Christ,
Who, in a human life, a human heart,
Didst show the world, and showest still the world,
The very heart and life of God Himself:

Christ,
Most perfect man,
And therefore perfect God:

Christ,
Most perfect God,
And therefore perfect man:

Christ,
The Goal of all our race's long advance,
Who in each heart, the Inward Christ, still strivest up
to God:

Christ,
Saviour, human Friend, and God most High,
Here is my heart, my life,
For Thee this day.

BÁBAR,
Emperor of Hindustan,
Being caught, with his army,
By a destroying blizzard on the Hindu Kush,
Came at last with his men to a little cave,
But would not himself be safe therein,
Because there was in it no space for his men:
Rather he chose to abide without, in the storm and the
frost,
With those whom he counted his brothers and friends.

So also,
O Master divine,
Thou dwellest not far and at ease in a lazy heaven:
But endurest with us, whom Thou countest Thy friends,
The brunt of the storm,
Bearing all that we bear,
Sharing the toil and the strife,
Steeling our hearts to be strong
By the joy of Thy presence.

HOW shall men stablish their rights?
How shall they combat the wrongs, black as night,
That crush down their lives in despair?
How shall they win, for the future,
That fuller and ampler life,
That radiant freedom, that joy,
Which now so sorely they lack?
How shall the Kingdom be built
Where none is oppressed or despised,
Where all men are brothers, and equal, and free?

We know not, O Master:—
This only we know,
We must follow Thy way, by Thy grace:
For over the passions and plottings of men,
As swiftly the centuries glide,
There looms for us, silent, compelling, Thy Cross.

All we know is Thy generous love,
Which recked not of insult and wrong to itself,

Nor of shame and despair:
Which forgave, and trusted, and toiled, to the dark bitter end
In humility, poverty, pain:
Which strove for the poor and the slave,
Forgetting itself:
Which sought not its own,
Neither justice, nor freedom, nor rights:
But laboured and died,
And, dying, forgave all the blackness of wrong it had borne;
Yet, so dying, built by its death
A Kingdom immortal of freedom and hope,
Wherein we, even we, may abide.

Teach us to work for that Kingdom,
O Master divine,
To work for its amplest coming on earth,
To tell men Thy goodness, Thy Love:
So that none may be ground in injustice and shame,
But all men be brothers, and equal, and free,
Because they know Thee,
Their Captain, their Saviour, their King,
Because they rejoice in Thy will and Thy way,
Which is freedom and friendship and hope.

SINFUL and vicious and base though this heart of
mine be,
Though I fall and am foul in the mire of shame:
Yet, patient and faithful for ever,
He raiseth me up.

In Him, and only in Him,
There is power for conquest and growth,
For the purging of filth when I fall,
For steeling this fickle and treacherous will to His
purpose of good.
In Him, and only in Him,
There is fulness of freedom and life,
There is beauty and joy.

Not by words does He work for the life of my soul,
Nor in precept and fiat and rite,
But in deed and in life and in love;

In deed, for He fights at my side:
When the foe is remorseless and fierce
'Tis His arm that protects me and wards off the blows;

In life, for His friendship is strong in my heart—
Not a story of old, nor a doctrine of priests,
But a fact in this everyday world, to be lived with and
used;

In love, for His heart is here now, close beating by mine,
Revealing the beauty of forest and star and of all He
has made,
Warm, intimate, close and familiar, faithful to death
and beyond.

IN weakness and fever and pain,
When dumbly a man abhors all that he is and has done,
When a horror of darkness covers his soul:
Then, Redeemer, O then, is Thy strength his stay.

In failure and shame and despair,
When a man is broken and lost,
When his soul knows well that the work of his life is in vain:
Then, Redeemer, O then, is Thy strength his stay.

In the deep black tides of a grief more bitter than death,
When a man is forsaken, bleeding and torn,
When his soul is shrivelled and seared in the thought of the years ahead:
Then, Redeemer, O then, is Thy strength his stay.

In the last grim issue of all, when life is a dream behind,
And my soul fares forth alone:
Then, Redeemer, O then, shall Thy saving strength be my stay,
And beholding the face of death I shall find there the face of my Friend.

FRIENDLESS were we, desolate and helpless,
When first we came unto Thee,
O Thou Who art all in all to our souls.

In the tempest, at blackest midnight,
The track of our lives was lost,
And we stumbled and fell in the miry fens of despair.

Then, oh then, didst Thou find us and save us:
Thanks be to Thee, Thou didst find us and save us.

And now, though the tempests rage,
Though the midnight be black, and the way mired deep,
We are confident, sure of our path, and strong.

We go forward with steady joy;
For now our hands are in Thine,
Thy love is around us, Thy guidance directs us,
The bliss of Thy presence
Changes darkness and danger, weariness, tempest and
death,
Into heaven on earth.

Thanks be to Thee, O Master, O Lover divine,
Thou didst find us and save us.

WE thank Thee, Father, that Thy poet-heart,
Striving to set in words Thy love for men,
Striving to tell to men the beauty and the joy
That dwell immortally in Thee,
Striving to show to men's dull eyes
Thy glory burning in Thy world
Chose thus the language of a Life,
Spake unto men in Man,
In Man, as these are, poor and desolate,
Full knowing all the aches of human wretchedness,
In hunger, thirst and weariness,
Misunderstood, reviled,
Buffeted, spat on, crucified.

Our God, we thank Thee for Thy Poem of that Life,
Thy word to men,
For this that sets eternally
Thy love, Thy beauty,
The splendour of Thy joy,
In speech for man.

Grant us the eyes, the ears, the hearts,
To read that Poem, and to comprehend,
To hear that Word, and act on it,
In lives of humble, gallant service done for Thee,
In lives of joyful comradeship with Christ.

OUT of the mire of sin and despair,
Out of the black abyss of the soul's dark night,
He guides us safe to His home.

Nought spares He Himself for our saving,
He bears the full brunt of the storm,
Dauntless He suffers the shame and the wounds.

O Saviour, we cannot reward Thee,
No guerdon of praise can we bring,
We are shamefast and voiceless before Thee.

Only, our hearts exult at Thy presence,
Our Hero, our Saviour, our God,
Who art Soul of all worlds,
And the solace and Joy of these narrow hearts.

XII.

IMMORTAL LIFE

A LITTLE thing is our earth,
Slung, by a thread unseen,
In a tiny trail round a lesser star:
Beyond it—Infinitude,
Universe beyond universe,
Bright, estranged, unknowable,

A little thing is our Earth,
And beyond it is Infinitude.

A little thing on our Earth is a home—
A home where love dwells and grows fairer day after day—
Beyond it are the unending multitudes,
The swarming millions of humanity,
Knowing and caring nought that it lives.

A little thing is a home,
And bounding it close is Death.

Yet the love that dwells there
Is not little,
Nor is it bounded by Death.
It is lord of all worlds:
Deathless it is, and incorruptible.

For life it is of God's Life,
Who is Love.

FATHER,
Again we look forth from our shelter in Thee,
At this holy hour of dawn, when we truly live,
To the day's long restless labour ahead:

From our mountain-eyrie
We gaze o'er the flats of monotonous labour,
To the mountains beyond:

Range beyond range they lie,
Those mountains,
How many they are we know not,
Yet this we know—each range is a refuge, a stronghold,
A strong defence of communion and peace:

And beyond, through the mists of the future,
Lie the ultimate peaks,
The goal of our journey at last,
Our Home,
Where face to face we shall see,
We shall see.

O GOD, our God,
We would live to-day by Thy life,
Be moved by Thy will,
Speak the words of Thy love unto men,
Step clear of this half-existence
Into life abundant, eternal
Of service for Thee.

ANOTHER day to be lived together,
Another day of labour, weariness, failure,
It may be, of danger or grief:
Yet another day of eternal life in God's heaven.

Another day to be lived together,
In the palace Thou, Father, hast given,
In this world of Thine, where all the day long
Thou art Thyself our Comrade, Protector, and Friend.

Another day of eternal life,
Life together, in service for God,
Upheld by His presence.

ACROSS the blackness of night
And the leagues of desolate forest
Shineth afar, from an unknown hill-top,
The flame of a beacon-fire.

Across the blackness of space,
Farther than thought can span,
Shineth afar, steady, unfailing,
The flame of a star.

The fire burns low,
Even the star shall die,
But across the waste of the empty years,
Love burns on, eternally,
In God Who kindled it.

WE thank Thee, O our God,
That, though our life
Is but a brief and flickering restlessness
Upon the permanence of things eternal,
Yet is the meaning and the value of it all,
The purpose whereunto the worlds have being,
Thy underlying Elder World,
Thus radiantly revealed:

We thank Thee, O our God,
That thus Thy heaven cuts across our own dark world
Closely indwelling it:

We thank Thee that Thy Truth thus underpins our truthlessness,
That what abides and stands
Thus stalwartly sustains our changefulness:
We thank Thee that in simplest things
We thus see manifest
Thy framework of reality:

We thank Thee that the beauty and the love
Of one small child
Can this convert and purify our gloomy souls,
Can teach them to behold and to adore unchanging Truth,
Can help them to reach our their arms to Thee,
Can make them apprehend eternal things,
Truth, goodness, beauty,
Can lead them forth safe to Thy deathless world.

WE praise Thee this day,
O Lover divine,
For the music and laughter and joy
Which are not of this world,
Which are surer and deeper, beyond all telling,
Than aught that this world can give.

We praise Thee this day
For the music and laughter and joy
Of Thine own eternal life:
For the heart overflowing with gladness
Because it has Thee:
For the zest and delight of the humblest life lived on earth
That is kindled aflame with the friendship of God.

Keep us this day in Thy friendship,
Give us union of heart and of will with Thyself.

DEATH

THE night is gone:
Slowly my soul, at peace,
Opens its eyes upon Thy face,
O God, who art more tender than a mother:
Slowly the knowledge grows in me that this is Thou
Slowly (as once in days gone by
My mother wakened me)
I know that what seemed pain,
Is but thy morning-kiss:
Slowly my soul responds, awakening gradually.

Then, in a flash,
The knowledge sweeps all shadows of the night away,
I am with Thee, for ever:
For ever one, in Thee, my Home,
With Thy pure company of loving souls.

SERENE and slow in the blue empyrean
The eagles wheel,
Aloof from the mists and the dust of the world:

So also our souls, O Father,
Would dwell in Thy realm of light and peace,
Unstained by the world's annoyance,
Unstirred by its petty spites, its lack of generous love:

Tear us, we pray Thee, remorselessly free
From all that keeps us apart from Thyself:

Give, by Thy Spirit, the strength we so sorely need
That our souls may soar unfettered aloft
To that radiant joyous realm
Where Thou reignest in bliss
Amongst all who have conquered hatred and given Thy Spirit free scope in their lives:

May our own true life be lived in that realm
Even now, when we strive and stumble and fail in this fog-bound world.

HOW glad shall we be to lay by,
On that great, dear day when we enter on life,
The wisdom of earth, which is ever more conscious of error,
The pleasure of earth, which is bitter as gall to the tasting,
The success of earth, which turns swiftly to dust and decay,
All this tawdry and threadbare cloak of existence,
All that we have and we are, save the things that abide,
Love given of God,
Simple joy in His beautiful world,
The glad sweet laughter of childhood.

IF it be joyful as this
To know Thee and live with Thee here on this earth,
O Lover divine,
Where our eyes are blinded
By the dust of the world,
And our ears are deafened
By its roaring traffic:

Ah what miracles of joy,
Unspeakable by human lips,
Unthinkable by human minds,
The veil of the future now conceals,
When at last we shall lay aside this feeble and narrow-souled being,
To be clothed, in death, with immortal youth.

Prepare us, we pray Thee, for that great day:
Teach us to live these common-place lives
In the glory of that eternal sunrise,
When we shall awaken from this sleep
And find ourselves gazing at last —
Drowsily at first, but then with what keen and thrilling
delight—
Into Thy eyes.

BLUE as the deep mid-ocean are the irises,
Blue as the deep mid-heaven are the irises,
In the rich green grass they stand like stars, innumerable.

Their beauty is an immortal thing,
Eternity o'ershadowing time,
Permanence o'ershadowing corruptibility,
Truth o'ershadowing delusion.

For the life of the Most High God, immortally,
Beats through the veins of transient materiality,
And wells forth
Into Beauty.

The vehicle of that loveliness shall perish,
The fragile structure of blossom and leaf,
The fair human form,
Even the snows on high shall be melted at last:

Yet their beauty abides for ever,
And ever more truly exists,
In God,
Who is Beauty and Love and Truth.

NEITHER in lfe nor in death is there aught to fear,
For love indwells and sustains the Whole.

In life there is nothing to fear,
For step by step, like little children,
We are led by Him who holdeth our hands,
By Him who hath crowned our lives, day by day,
With His wonders of beauty and love and delight.

In death there is nothing to fear,
For, there also, love is supreme,
There also God's hand shall guide us, as little children.

Death is naught but the passage at last
From this our darkness and gloom to yonder splendour
of light,
From this our half-knowledge, half-friendship, half-
goodness,
To that perfection:
From this our death
To that fulness and freedom of life.

THOU hast but to listen,
And thou shalt hear Him:
He speaketh aloud in the wind of evening,
In the joyful gladness of children, the song of the birds.

In the dayspring upon the forest
Is His face clear seen.

Aye, and in the darkness,
In the black and dreadful midnight,
Stretch forth thy hand,
And thou shalt clasp Him.

Round about His Love encompassing
Hour by hour sustains thee.

Thou hast but to be silent:
Thou hast but to receive
With simple-hearted trust
The boon ineffable, immortal,
Which He is waiting to bestow.

Oh, be still, my soul,
Receive Him:
And even here and now
Thou shalt know eternal life.

FRAIL is this human flesh,
Easy to be shattered in a moment,
Easy to be wasted by disease,
At the last sure-fated to corruption.

Even as a flower
The lovelier it be is the less enduring,
The more delicate and fragile,
So also is this human flesh.

Beautiful it is beyond all telling,
Gracious, tender and resplendent:
It revealeth unto men the beauty and the love of God,
Yet swiftly it perisheth in shame.

Swiftly is its beauty but decay,
Its grace, its splendour, change to nameless horror.

Nay: the flesh may perish,
But the beauty is immortal,
The love, the grace, the tenderness
Are eternal things,
For they are God incarnate once again:
And, though the flesh may perish, they endure in God.

HERE, in the velvet Indian night,
Will we swim for awhile,
Sure-clasped in the silken embrace of the water:

Warm and soft is its touch
As the cheek of a sleeping child,
Cool also it is, delicious and goodly,
After the day's long heats.

Above us the great stars burn,
Huge, passionate, splendid:
Around us the dark hills sleep in their silence,
Instinct with the calm and the power of God.

From afar comes faintly the cry of a bird:
And, see, in the East,
A silvery radiance heralds the moon.

Softly there passes beyond us, and dies,
A tiny breeze from the shore,
Bearing the scent of flowers,
Ruffling the waters but for an instant.

Here in the midst of the lake
Let us lie for awhile,
Hands under head, scarce a ripple marring reluctant
The faint star-sheen on the shadowy water.

Let us gaze and gaze
Deep, deep in the lustrous eternity above us:—
And know once more
Whence we come, and whither we go.

SOME day, O Father,
When this my steady-beating heart is still,
This body broken,
I shall be one with these—

One shall I be, in Thee, O Death-destroyer,
With wind and sea and stars,
These silent, stately-wheeling stars:

One shall I be, in Thee, O Life-bestower,
With dawn and evening,
With all things simple, lovely, pure:

Oh purge me, Lord of life and death:
Make clean my heart for that great day of life,
Make keen my will to follow Thine
Across the bars of death:

Here, in this morning silence,
Is all I have and am
For Thee --
Is all I have and am,
In this half life and that full life beyond,
For Thee, my God.

NO sadness is there, nor care,
For those that love Him:
Suffer they may, die they must,
Yet trusting and holding Him,
They are content.

For His love is stronger than death,
More patient than pain:
When my soul shall escape from the final shattering agony,
Then, ah then, shall He put forth His might,
And make me His own for ever.

Must I wait till that day?
Nay, one thing alone do I need,
That, a little child,
Here and now I may put forth my hand in the darkness,
And be grasped by His love—

Grasped, did I say?
Nay, my soul shall be stormed,
Mastered with strength resistless,
Garrisoned fast by the armies of God,
By immortal and heavenly joy in His love.

THOU art our peace, O Lord.
From all these thousand wearinesses of daily life,
From disillusionments and disappointments,
From nervous hurry, from breathless and senseless haste,
We turn to Thee, and are at peace.

In a moment all the clamour dies,
The bonds fall off,
The clinging distractions are all shaken loose,
And our shrivelled souls expand exulting
In the sunshine of Thy presence.

In a moment this earth-life is far behind us,
And we tread the cool, spacious, peaceful hills of Thy eternity,
Where in quiet content our souls hold converse with Thyself.

Soon we must return to the labour and the din,
Yet on our brows, we pray Thee, set the seal of our
home,
That home whence we come,
Wherein day by day we live our true lives,
Whither some day we return joyfully for ever—
That home which is Thyself.